LUTON TOWN FC

A SEASON BY SEASON HISTORY
1885 – 2018

GEORGE JACKSON

THANKS

My sincere thanks are due to to Roger Wash and Simon Pitts for their excellent publication *Luton Town Football Club The Full Record,* which has been the source of both inspiration and much information, to my son Bill and his wife June for buying me that book for Christmas, to my brother Nigel for being my companion and chauffeur to Hatters games whenever they have played within a reasonable distance from us in recent years and finally to Nathan Jones and his team for winning promotion and providing me with an appropriate place to stop (or at least pause) this history. Thank you all.

George W H Jackson 2018

NOTE

All refences to appearances and goals scored include substitute appearances and relate to all league, non-league and cup competitions unless otherwise stated.

LUTON TOWN F.C. - A SEASON BY SEASON HISTORY

SEASON 1885-86

Luton Town Football Club was formed by an amalgamation of Luton's two top teams, Luton Excelsior and Luton Wanderers, which was agreed at a public meeting on 11th April 1885. Friendly games were played by invitation with the first competitive game being a 3-0 defeat away to Great Marlow in the First Round of the FA Cup played on 31st October 1885. Marlow were a strong team having been semi-finalists only three years before. Now known as Marlow Town they are the only club to have applied to enter the FA Cup in every year since the competition's inception. In July 2010, Luton played a friendly with Marlow to celebrate the 125th anniversary of that first competitive game. The Hatters played in their original strip of pink and navy halved shirts and navy blue shorts. This time Luton ran out winners 3-1.

SEASON 1886-87

Part of the amalgamation agreement had been the use of Excelsior's pitch on an enclosed field off Dallow Lane (now Dallow Road) and this continued to be the venue for friendly games against teams invited by letter or found through advertisements placed in sporting magazines. Opponents included some of the best teams in the country such as Hendon, St Albans, Old Etonians and Hotspur.

The only competitive game of the season was against Hotspur at Dallow Lane in the FA Cup First Round where they were beaten 3-1. Hotspur would of course be known later as Tottenham Hotspur. The first ever game for Town was a friendly at home against Higham Ferrers and their first ever goal was scored by J C 'Charlie' Lomax who had played for both Wanderers and Excelsior and was instrumental in the amalgamation. His brother D A N 'Dan' Lomax also played for Luton and was killed in action when a Captain in the 1st Welch Regiment in the South African War.

SEASON 1887-88

Once again the FA Cup was the only competitive game and once again it was First Round defeat this time away to Chatham with a disappointing 5-1 scoreline. The game was watched by 800 spectators, less than the estimated 1,000 at Dallow Road for the previous season's tie against Hotspur. The club was run and the team was picked by a small committee who often selected some of their number to play.

SEASON 1888-89

Finally Luton managed a win in the FA Cup but didn't even get to Round 1 as there were now qualifying rounds. There was a comfortable 4-0 win at home to Reading in Qualifying Round 1. In Q2 a 3-3 draw at Chesham was followed by a 10-2 win in the replay with Thring and G Deacon both scoring hat-tricks.

Unfortunately in Q3 Town went down 3-1 at home to Old Brightonians. The game against Reading saw the debut of L C R Thring whose father J C Thring had been one of those who in 1848 drew up the Cambridge Rules of Football which later became the template for- the first set of rules produced by the Football Association. Leonard Thring had moved to the area to become the first Headmaster of Dunstable Grammar School (my old school) when it opened in 1888. He played regularly for Luton until the club turned professional after which he often acted as referee and was Headmaster at DGS until 1921.

SEASON 1889-90

There was little of note other than that in the FA Cup an away win at Maidenhead was followed by a 4-0 defeat away to Old St Pauls. Elsewhere, civil engineer John Brodie of Liverpool, who would later be responsible for the Mersey Tunnel, invented goal nets. Nets would not become compulsory in the league until 1891 and not until 1894 in the FA Cup thereby ending all disputes as to which side of a post a ball had passed and less work for the 'Umpires' as referee's assistants were called.

SEASON 1890-91

Luton Town became semi-professional when the committee agreed to pay three players five shillings a week from December 1890 – not a fortune, about £30 at today's value.

Professionalism had been legal since 1885 but was mainly a 'northern thing' although many clubs paid 'expenses'. Luton were the first club in the south of England to pay their players. It didn't seem to help things on the pitch as in their only competitive game Town lost 7-0 at home to the 93rd Highland Regiment in the 1st Qualifying Round of the FA Cup.

SEASON 1891-92

From August 1891, the whole team were on a weekly wage and a number of prominent amateur players including the three Lomax brothers, L C R Thring and G W Barrett ceased to turn out. It may or may not have been coincidence but the professional era saw Luton's best ever run to date in the FA Cup. There were home wins against Swindon Town 4-3 and Windsor Phoenix Athletic 3-0 followed by away wins at two Bristol teams, Bedminster 4-1 and Clifton 3-0. The run came to an end when Luton lost 3-0 to Middlesborough at Dallow Lane (by now known locally as Town Meadow) where the attendance was estimated at 4,000. This was the first season that the rules of football allowed for penalty kicks. One of the advantages of professionalism was that the club was now able to buy the players shirts. Previously they had to buy their own which perhaps accounts for the variations in tone in early black and white team photographs.

SEASON 1892-93

Three players in the FA Cup teams had not played for Luton in that competition before but nevertheless two wins were achieved. There were home wins 4-1 against Old St. Marks and 4-0 versus Old Etonians before a 4-2 defeat away to Polytechnic in the 3rd Qualifying Round. Polytechnic were originally known as Hanover United when formed in the 1870s in Chiswick and are said to be the first club to use 'United' in their name. They changed their name to Polytechnic at the start of this 1892 season and still exist.

SEASON 1893-94

Luton were excused the 1st Qualifying Round of the FA Cup and then had wins 1-0 away to Old Westminsters and 5-1 at home to Norwich CEYMS before a tie against the 1st Sherwood Foresters.The game was played at Colchester, presumanbly at the barracks, and Luton were leading 4-2 after 24 minutes of extra time when the referee abandoned the game and recorded the full-time score of 2-2 as the result. Justice was done with Town winning 2-1 in the home replay .In the 1st Round proper they were drawn away to Middlesborough Ironopolis and lost 2-1.

Norwich CEYMS (Church of England Young Mens Society) FC still exist and play in the Anglia Combination. Middlesborough Ironopolis (as opposed to Middlesborough) only existed for five years playing at the Paradise Ground but in that short time won the Northern League three times and reached the quarter-finals of the FA Cup.

A former Ironopolis player, Scotsman Hugh Galbraith, made his Luton debut this season on transfer from Burnley and would score 33 goals in just 46 appearances. Glasgow born John Finlayson also joined having previously been at Middlesborough, Bootle and Ardwick (Manchester City). They probably weren't lonely as in the following season they were joined at Luton by a McCartney, a McCrindle and a McEwan.

SEASON 1894-95

The Southern League was formed and Luton were invited to become founder members of Division One. There were only nine teams in the division which included Millwall Athletic, Swindon Town, Southampton St Marys, Reading, Royal Ordnance Factories and Clapton. Town used eighteen players during the sixteen match season and Hugh Galbraith top scored with 12 goals. By this time Luton were wearing navy shorts and red/maroon shirts with an eight-pointed star badge. Luton's final league position was 2nd some way behind Champions Millwall and they also had a reasonable run in the FA Cup with a home win 8-2 against City Ramblers and away wins 6-1 at St Albans and 2-0 at Ilford. Tottenham Hotspur were beaten 4-0 at Dallow Lane in a replay following a 2-2 draw away but in the 1st Round proper defeat came at home at the hands of Football League side Preston North End.

SEASON 1895-96

There was one additional team in the Division and Luton lost only one home game. They were unbeaten in the last eight games which included some emphatic victories at Dallow Lane, Swindon 7-1, Chatham 9-1, New Brompton 8-1 and Clapton beaten 6-0 both home and away. Despite this form, Luton still finished 2nd again behind Millwall Athletic. There was no progress in the FA Cup with Spurs getting revenge for the previous season with a 2-1 win in the 1st Qualifying Round. The season's top scorer was again Hugh Galbraith with 17 goals from 16 appearances. By way of (not much) consolation, Town won the Luton Charity Cup.

SEASON 1896-97

Having twice been in second place, Luton resigned from the Southern League in August 1896 and applied to join the Football League. Unfortunately their application was rejected and they were forced to play a season in just the United League. The United League was actually just formed this season to provide additional mid-week fixtures for teams from a number of leagues and ran in this format until 1901-02 when it ceased operation. It was re-formed in 1905-06 purely for entry by Southern League clubs and ran until 1908-09. Luton remained members until 1906-07. In the United League this season,opponents included local clubs Rushden, Wellingborough and Kettering but also Woolwich Arsenal and Tottenham Hotspur. Luton came second in this eight team league behind (you've guessed it) Millwall Athletic.

In the FA Cup there were wins at home 7-0 against the 1st Scots Guards, 5-0 away to Marlow and 3-0 at home to Tottenham. In the 1st Round proper Luton went out 1-0 to West Bromwich Albion watched by a record crowd of 6,898 at Dallow Lane. Two months later, on 3rd April 1897, Town moved to a new ground at Dunstable Road.

SEASON 1897-98

Luton applied once more to join the Football League and this time were succesful playing their first ever game in the League on 4th September recording a 1-1 draw away at Leicester Fosse (later Leicester City) in Division 2. The squad had been strengthened with James 'Punch' McEwan, who would win the FA Cup with Bury in 1903, coming in from Everton. Glasgow born John McCartney, who had played well over 100 games for Newton Heath came in for just one season but would return in 1927 as Luton's first ever manager. Also from Scotland and also previously at Newton Heath was Bob Donaldson who would score 10 goals in 17 starts in his only season. Another Glaswegian, Tom McInnes, who had one Scottish cap came from Everton and with 10 goals was joint top league scorer with Donaldson and William S Stewart. McInnes would stay with Luton until he retired in 1900 after 43 goals in 153 appearances and Stewart would make 105 appearances with 38 goals in two spells at Luton.

The Hatters were now up with the bigger boys and opponents included Newton Heath (Manchester United), Manchester City, Small Heath (Birmingham City), Newcastle United, Burnley and Blackpool.

Luton's best results were however at home against such teams as Gainsborough Trinity 4-0, Lincoln City 9-3, Grimsby Town, 6-0, Loughborough 7-0 and Walsall 6-0 ensuring a mid-table 8th in the sixteen team league.

In th FA Cup, Luton were drawn against Tottenham Hotspur yet again beating them 4-3 at White Hart Lane and then winning 2-0 at Clapton before going out 1-0 to Bolton Wanderers at Dunstable Road. Competing in the United League, now extended to nine clubs, Luton were champions finally beating Millwall Athletic to the top spot. Perhaps their luck had changed with the new strip adopted for Division 2, black,red and white striped shirts and navy blue shorts.

SEASON 1898-99

Life in the league was more of a struggle this season and ended in a disappointing 13th place. Among the few bright spots were home wins against Darwen 8-1 and Barnsley 4-1 but Luton only won two away games in the league conceding five or more goals on six occasions, the worst being a 9-0 demolition in Birmingham against Small Heath. In the United League, which now had eleven members, the decline was even more dramatic. With just two wins and three draws, Luton went from first to rock bottom last. One other bright spot was the emergence of Luton born winger Arthur 'Jimmy' Durrant, who had been signed from Luton Stanley in 1897. He made 140 league appearances for Town, moving to Leicester Fosse in 1904 where he made exactly the same number. He returned to Luton in 1913-14 and retired with a final tally for Luton of 47 goals in 199 appearances.

The qualifying rounds of the FA Cup saw the first competitive meeting with the team we love to hate, Watford. A 2-2 draw at home on 29th October was followed by a 1-0 replay win in Watford. Originally Watford Rovers and then South Hertfordshire, they had merged with Watford St Marys to become Watford only that year and were not yet at Vicarage Road. Next there was a 4-3 home win against Shepherds Bush (whose ground would be taken over by Queens Park Rangers) followed by three games against perennial cup opponents Tottenham in the 5th Qualifying Round. There were 1-1 draws home and away before Spurs won the 2nd replay 2-0. This game was played at the home of Tufnell Park FC who were then one of the top amateur teams in the country.

SEASON 1899-1900

Form slumped even further in Division 2. There were five good wins, all at home, 5-2 against Burton Swifts, 4-0 versus Walsall, 3-0 against Barnsley and 4-0 versus both Gainsborough Trinity and Loughborough but these were the only wins home or away. Not quite so many goals were conceded away as last season but 6-0 at Sheffield Wednesday and 7-3 in the return game at Walsall stand out in a season that left Town 17th and last but one. Luton did not compete in the United League this season and there was little joy in the FA Cup. Lowestoft Town were beaten away and Watford 3-2 at home but after a 1-1 draw at Dunstable Road, Luton were dumped out 4-1 by Queens Park Rangers. One significant debut was made when Luton boy Fred Hawkes made two league appearances and scored once.

Hawkes would go on to make 625 appearances, mostly in midfield and become Luton's all-time record holder in this respect. It would have been even higher had his career not been interupted by WW1 and he is probably the first to qualify as a 'Luton Legend'.

Having finished 17th, Luton would need to seek re-election to the Football League. They decided not to do so instead seeking re-admittance to the now much stronger Southern League. This was agreed and Town would start next season as a non-league club again. The decision was due to 'financial problems' which were affecting the club, possibly not for the first time but certainly not for the last. Attendances had slumped, player's wages were higher and there were the costs involved in moving to a new ground just two seasons before but a major factor was travel costs. Of the seventeen other clubs in Division 2 only Woolwich Arsenal were from the South of England, six were from the Midlands and the rest were from the North. Travel distances were therefore considerable.

SEASON 1900-01

Back in the Southern League Division One and wearing the new kit adopted the season before of navy blue shirts with a white pinstripe and shield shaped LTFC badge and with white shorts, Luton faced some familiar teams and some new ones including both Bristol City and Bristol Rovers for the first time in a league situation. The season could be described as 'steady' with the high and the low probably coming in successive games – a 5-2 home win against Gravesend followed by a 5-0 defeat at Southampton.

They finished 11th out of fifteen and the furthest they had to travel north was to Kettering Town. In a seven team United League, Luton were runner-up to Rothwell.

There had been something of a clear-out and only eight of the twentyfive players used in the previous season were retained. There was one interesting signing among the newcomers, James Blessington born in Linlithgow came in from Bristol City. He had previously spent six seasons with Celtic where he had won three league titles and been capped four times by Scotland. He would score 38 times for Luton in 104 appearances before leaving for Leicester in 1903. At Leicester he would later become their player-manager and then their first ever manager. There was a mini-run in the FA Cup with a 4-1 win at Kings Lynn followed by home wins against the Civil Service 9-0 and Queens Park Rangers 3-0 before going out 2-0 to Bristol City also at home.

SEASON 1901-02

There were now sixteen teams in the league and Luton, wearing their new pale blue shirts with white shorts, achieved a comfortable 7th place with no spectacular scores, the best performance being 4-2 away at Northampton Town. The FA Cup however was a different story and a club scoring record was set when Apsley were beaten 13-1 in the 1st qualifying round at Dunstable Road. Wins followed against Bedford Queens Works at home, Lowestoft Town and Watford away and QPR at home. Luton were then watched by 10,000, probably the biggest crowd they had experienced so far in their history when they held Woolwich Arsenal away 1-1. Unfortunately the replay resulted in defeat 2-0.

Two more 'legendary' players made their debut in this season. Luton born Herbert Moody was a youth player with Luton Stanley when he signed in 1901. He moved to Leicester Fosse for two seasons but came back to Luton in 1907. By the time he left for Millwall in 1912 he had scored 106 goals in 266 appearances.His goal tally gives him 5th place in Luton's all-time list. Bob Hawkes (no relation to Fred) was born near Hitchin and came through as a Luton youth player playing on the wing. He was the first Luton player to be capped by England while playing for the club, winning 19 England Amateur caps before five full international caps caps in 1907-08 and being an important member of England's succesful team at the 1908 Olympic Games. In his career with Town, which lasted until 1920, he made 410 appearances and scored 48 goals. Had his career not been affected by the war he would have been higher than his 10th place in all-time appearances for Luton.

SEASON 1902-03

A not very eventful season with Luton ending the season in 11th place. There were 4-0 home wins against Northampton Town and West Ham United and the double was achieved over Watford with a 4-1 win at Dunstable Road. Central defender Fred White played in every game league and cup as he had also done in the previous season. White, born in Dunstable, signed for Luton as a 20yr old in 1900 and stayed with the club until his retirement in 1909 by which time he had made 304 appearances and scored 15 goals. Also ever-present was Jim Blessington, Fred Hawkes missed only one game and 'Jimmy' Durrant only two.

In the FA Cup a 3-0 win at Loftus Road against QPR was followed by home wins against Lowestoft Town 5-1, Fulham 5-1 and Kidderminster Harriers 3-0 before exit 3-0 away to Millwall in the 1st Round proper.

SEASON 1903-04

There was a slight improvement in league position up to 8th and no prolific goal scoring by Luton or their opponents with the highest league score in 34 matches being three and that being achieved only five times (three for, two against). Only seventeen players were used all season and two of those only played one game. Goalkeeper F Thompson played every league and cup game in his only season at the club and Fred Hawkes was also ever-present. J W Bennett missed only one game in his only season at the club, Thomas Allsopp played 35 in his last season with Luton and Jimmy McEwan thirtyfour. McEwan transferred in from Bury for his second spell at Luton and would go on to make 175 appearances. Tommy Allsopp played first class cricket as a bowler for Leicestershire and MCC. He served in WW1 reaching the rank of Sergeant and survived only to die in the flu epidemic of 1918 when in his early 40s.

The FA Cup saw home wins against Hitchin Town 2-1 and Watford who were at the wrong end of Luton's highest score of the season 4-1. Defeat followed in the 5th Qualifying Round 3-1 at Fulham. Luton continued to wear the strip of pale blue shirts, white shorts and navy blue socks but the shirts were of unusual design having no collars and looking like a long-sleeved T shirt.

SEASON 1904-05

Despite some good performances at home, against Portsmouth 4-3, Northampton Town 4-2, Swindon Town 4-1, Wellingborough 4-0 and Fulham 6-0 this was Luton's worst season since returning to the Southern League finishing in 17th place. Eight players played 30 or more games in a settled side, Fred Hawkes, Jimmy McEwan, goalkeeper W Lindsay and Fred White being amongst them. Three of these regulars Davie Ross (top scorer with 12), Ted Turner and George Lamberton were at Luton for just this season but one was much more interesting, W E 'Billy' Barnes who was signed from West Ham United. Barnes had previously won the FA Cup with Sheffield United scoring the winning goal in a replayed final. Billy made 134 appearances for Luton, scoring 17 goals before moving to Queens Park Rangers. He made 234 league turn-outs for QPR and is included in their list of 100 all-time greats. When his playing career ended he went into management and won the Copa del Rey three times between 1915 and 1921 for Athletic Bilbao.

Luton's only FA Cup tie ended in a 4-0 defeat away to Fulham. The Dunstable Road ground was needed for housing development and the last game of the season on 25th April, a 2-0 win against Reading, saw the end of this chapter and the next season would be at the new stadium built a few hundred yards away at Kenilworth Road.

SEASON 1905-06

The first league game at Kenilworth Road was a 0-0 draw with Plymouth Argyle but it was the start of a much better season and a 4th place finish. Again, a number of players came into the club for just one or two seasons but there were some notable signings. Alexander 'Sandy' Brown, who had won his only Scottish cap in 1904, signed from Middlesborough. He would top score this season with 18 goals in 31 league games and in his Luton career would score 47 goals from just 96 appearances in all competitions. Defender W 'Bill' McCurdey came from Tottenham for his second spell at Luton and would take his appearances to 251 before retiring. Goalkeeper Peter Platt was signed from Liverpool and would appear between the sticks 183 times for Town and score a goal, a penalty at Leyton in 1908.

Again there was no success in the FA Cup with a defeat 1-0 away to Crystal Palace in the first ever meeting between the clubs. The United League was back in operation and Luton finished 4th of ten teams behind champions Watford. Bottom of the table were Southern United, a London club that entered the Southern League Div 2 and the London League this season for the first time. They left the Southern League at the end of the season and the London League part-way through the next and were never heard of again.

SEASON 1906-07

Despite some horrendous away results, losing at Sunderland 4-0, West Ham 5-1, Millwall 5-1 and Reading 7-2, two good home wins 5-3 against Leyton and a revenge 6-2 versus Swindon Town, together with some steady if unspectacular results, saw Luton once again in 4th spot. There was one notable signing, Abraham 'Abe' Jones, a central defender had played over 100 league games for both West Bromwich and Middlesborough and would play 166 times for Luton. His son Abe Jnr also played league football in the 1920s. More journeyman professionals came in for one or two seasons. Among these was full back Bert Jackson who has the honour of being the first Luton player to share my surname. Sandy Brown was again top scorer with 15 and no-one else made double figures. Bob Hawkes became the first Luton player to win a full England cap when he turned out against Northern Ireland at Goodison Park, Everton.

In the FA Cup there was a goal-less draw at Gainsborough Trinity with Luton winning the home replay 2-1. Sunderland were the next opponents at Kenilworth Road and for the first time the five figure attendance figure was reached as 10,500 watched a 0-0 draw. This was dwarfed by the 18,000 at Roker Park for the replay which Sunderland won 1-0. Town competed for the last time in the United League finishing third behind Crystal Palace and Brighton & Hove Albion with Watford in eighth (last) place.

SEASON 1907-08

Not a season to be remembered with Luton slumping to 18th place in the Southern League Div 1. Sandy Brown played only a handful of games and failed to score in his last season at the club and the top scorer with 12 was Luton boy Herbert Moody who came back from Leicester Fosse for a second spell at Kenilworth Road. The only signing of note was Bruce Rankin who had played six seasons for Everton and had been a crowd favourite at the Hawthorns with West Bromwich Albion. There were some thumping away defeats, 4-0 at Swindon, 5-0 at Leyton and 6-1 at Norwich with only a 4-0 home defeat of Crystal Palace to set against them. The FA Cup was even more of a disaster when Fulham came to Kenilworth Road and went away with an 8-3 win.

With the demise of the United League, Luton joined the Western League for additional games. Formed in 1892 as the Bristol & District League, it became the Western League in 1895. The only west team in the league however was Bristol Rovers and Luton's other opponents were Reading and four London clubs, West Ham, Crystal Palace, Millwall and Tottenham Hotspur. Town ended exactly mid-table with 12 points from twelve games.

SEASON 1908-09

Again there were some high scoring away defeats, 6-0 at Southampton, 4-0 at West Ham, 4-1 at Swindon, 4-0 at Queens Park Rangers and 5-2 at Coventry but this season there was better overall form and some good home wins as well, 4-0 against Norwich, 5-1 versus Portsmouth, 4-1 against Crystal Palace and 6-1 against Coventry. The end result was an improvement to a top-half finish in 9th place. Fred Hawkes and Abe Jones played all 40 league games. Stalwarts Bob Hawkes, Bill McCurdey and Herbert Moody all played over 30 as did three other players who had come in for just one of two seasons. These were mostly players coming towards the end of their careers and stepping down from league football. Typical ,of these was centre forward Alex Menzies who came from Manchester United where he won his one Scottish cap. One signing, winger Harold Stansfield played almost every game and would go on to appear 154 times and score 28 goals

The FA Cup 5th Qualifying Round saw a 1-1 draw at Kenilworth Road against Southend United. The replay also ended 1-1 after 90 minutes but extra time saw a goalfest with Luton winning 4-2. In the 1st Round proper, Town went down at home 2-1 to Millwall. Luton again competed in the Western League where West Ham, Millwall and Spurs had been replaced by Leyton, QPR and Croydon Common. The changes made no difference at Luton again finished 4th and again had 12 points from 12 games. Croydon Common, originally an amateur club had turned professional in 1907 and played in both divisions of the Southern League. They folded in 1917 and became the only Southern League team not to return to action after the war.

SEASON 1909-10

There were some reasonable home performances with 4-1 wins against Millwall and Coventry and 4-2 versus West Ham, Brentford and Watford but away form was a problem with defeats 6-0 at Norwich and 6-2 at Coventry with no less than six other teams putting four past keeper Richard Jarvis who was first choice now that Peter Platt had left the club. The backbone of the team continued to be Fred Hawkes, Bob Hawkes, Abe Jones and Herbert Moody. Centre-half Jones was only 5'7" but was said to miss very little in the air and Fred Hawkes was ever-present for the fourth consecutive season showing amazing fitness. Twelve of the 21 players used were new signings and few made much of a contribution. The exceptions were full back Edward Potts and winger Ernie Coxhead who would both go on to make more than 100 appearances for Luton and two forwards Tommy Quinn who played in all 42 league games and scored 21 goals and John Smith who scored 17 from 39 starts. Both would play one further season at Kenilworth Road. There was no involvement in any other league this season and a 2-1 defeat at Brentford was the only FA Cup game played.

SEASON 1910-11

A new season and a (nearly) new strip – the pale blue shirts now had a navy vee, the shorts were still white and this new style would last ten years as had the previous one. For the fifth season running Fred Hawkes played in every league and cup game. Bob Hawkes was still there as was Herbert Moody who had a new lease of life, top scoring with 24 goals in league and cup.

Centre-half Abe Jones had gone and was replaced by new signing Willie Bushell from Norwich City who now features in that club's one hundred best players list. Four other new players would stay for at least a second season including Tom Naisby who came in from South Shields to replace Jarvis as first choice goalkeeper. One who would only stay two seasons was Robbie Walker from Millwall who played the last ten games of the campaign scoring 4 goals but only 9 in 29 the next season before departing for Bristol Rovers where he would make over 100 appearances. Alexander McDonald came back from Croydon Common for a second spell at Luton but played only one game. There were some good home wins 4-0 against Bristol Rovers and Portsmouth, 4-1 against Leyton and 4-2 versus Coventry with an away win 4-1 at Southend. A few less nasty away defeats were recorded, 4-1 at Swindon. 4-2 at Exeter and Bristol Rovers and 4-0 at Plymouth. The end result was an improved 9th place.

The FA Cup 4th Qualifying Round was supposed to be played at Cambridge but for some reason it was played at Luton 'by arrangement'. Not a good decision for United as Luton won 9-1. In the next round it took a home replay to dispose of Rochdale 3-2 but in the 1st Round proper, Town came a cropper 5-1 at Northampton Town. Before the season ended both top scorers from the previous year, John Smith and Tommy Quinn were sold to Millwall for a joint fee of £300. Was this when Luton first gained a reputation as a 'selling club'?

SEASON 1911-12

Nine new players made their debut but for three their first game was their last, two played only twice and eight of the nine totalled only 25 games between them. Fred Hawkes, Bob Hawkes and keeper Tom Naisby were ever-present in all 39 games. Willie Bushell and Ernie Coxhead missed only one, Herbert Moody and Edward Potts two and Sammy Wightman was in his 35th game when disaster struck. In the game at Brighton on 8th April, Wightman was accidentally kicked in the stomach and died four days later of peritonitis. The last game of the season on 27th April 1912 marked quite an achievement for Fred Hawkes, he had played in every competitive game for Luton since 14th April 1906, ever-present for six years and 253 consecutive games. He missed very few before or after these dates and his final tally was 625 games, mostly at wing-half but occasionally up front. His last game would be in May 1920 and doubtless he would have played even more games had WW1 not interupted proceedings. Despite the efforts of Hawkes and the rest and a 7-1 win against Reading in the penultimate game of the season, Luton finished 19th and were relegated to Division 2 of the Southern League. They did no better in the FA Cup going out 4-2 at home to Notts County in their only game.

SEASON 1912-13

Down in Division 2 Luton virtually needed a season ticket to the Principality as no less than ten of their twelve opponents in the league were Welsh.

In addition to the usual suspects were Mardy, Mid-Rhondda, Aberdare, Treharris, Pontypridd, Llanelly and Ton Pentre. The only English Clubs were Southend United and Croydon Common. Despite their lowly status, Luton still attracted crowds averaging 5,000 to Kenilworth Road but this was dwarfed by the massive 22,000 at Cardiff where Luton lost 3-0 to City despite an earlier 2-0 win in the reverse fixture. No less than seventeen new players joined the squad including two who would share goalkeeping duties for the season. Most of the rest played only a few games and only two were significant, John Elvey who would make 125 appearances at full-back and Arthur 'Nippy' Wileman who was signed from Chelsea and would score 58 goals in 107 appearances for Town. John 'Jimmie' Chipperfield, signed from Luton Clarence, played only four games but didn't join the circus as he later played for Tottenham and Notts County. Luton finished 5th behind champions Cardiff City.

This season, Luton also competed in the Southern Alliance, a mid-week 'first team' league and came 3rd of nine clubs, all of which were English except Cardiff City who, somewhat strangely were last in this league. The FA Cup saw a 3-0 home win against Tunbridge Wells Rangers and then defeat 2-0 away at Croydon Common

SEASON 1913-14

A record breaking promotion season starting with seven straight wins and finishing with sixteen games undefeated and a record of W24 D3 L3 but still only 2nd place behind Mardy.

Some good signings had helped, A F 'Jimmy' Durrant came back for a second spell at Luton having been at Leicester Fosse and Leyton and would end his career with 47 goals from the wing in 199 games. Centre-half Robert Frith would make 80 appearances before the war came and F Rollinson would score 43 goals in 79 games in the same period. Ernie Simms came in from Barnsley and would score 130 goals from 189 appearances before and after the war in extraordinary circumstances. Sid W Hoar, a Leagrave youth player made his debut on the wing and would make 244 appearances before and after the conflict before being sold to Arsenal in 1924 for £3,000 and making over 100 starts there. Towards the end of the season, the Kenilworth Road attendance record was beaten again when 12,500 saw a 2-1 win against promotion rivals Stoke.

There were goals galore at Kenilworth Road with Luton beating Treharris 6-0, Abertillery 6-0, Mid-Rhondda 8-1, Aberdare 7-0, Caerphilly 4-0, Llanelly 5-1 and Swansea Town 5-0. Aberdare and Caerphilly were both hammered on their own grounds 5-1 and 9-0 respectively. Ernie Simms hit the back of the net 28 times in just 24 league games and Arthur Wileman also scored 28 from 27 appearances. Frank Rollinson scored 17 which would have been enough for top spot in many other seasons. All three were also prolific in the Southern Alliance scoring 22 between them despite not appearing in every match and helping Town to runner-up spot in this competition also behind Brighton. In the FA Cup a 3-0 home win against Croydon Common was followed by defeat 2-0 at South Shields in a replay after a 0-0 at home. Off the pitch, in February 1914, a fire was reported at the Great Northern Inn in Bute Street where the Licencee was Henry Stansfield who between 1908 and 1912 had scored 28 goals for Luton in 154 appearances on the left wing. He was unhurt.

SEASON 1914-15

Back in Division 1 of the Southern League, goals were not so easy to come by. Ernie Simms got 30 goals but eight of these were in the FA Cup and Rollinson and Wileman managed only 23 between them. The only scores of note were 4-2 home wins against both Gillingham and Watford and these were offset against defeats away 5-1 at Norwich and 4-0 at Reading. There were seven new signings including winger Hugh Roberts who was ever-present in his only season at the club, full-back John Dunn and forward Arthur Roe who would both be among the few still playing for the club after the war with Roe making 138 appearances. The 4th Qualifying Round of the FA Cup saw a club record broken when Great Yarmouth visited Kenilworth Road to be beaten 15-0 with Simms and Rollinson both scoring four. A narrow win at Oxford City was followed by a 5-1 scoreline at home to Bromley before defeat 3-0 away at Southampton

War had been declared on 28 July 1914 and it was somewhat controversial that league football had continued. Many worthies such as Sir Arthur Conan Doyle were suggesting that perhaps fit young men should be chasing the enemy rather than a football and it was even thought that the King could resign as President of the Football Association. To stem this criticism it was suggested that a footballers 'Pals' battalion should be formed and as a result William Joynson-Hicks MP convened a meeting at Fulham Town Hall on 12th December 1914 with the purpose of forming such a battalion to be known as the 17th (Service) Battalion Middlesex Regiment.

Several Luton players expressed an interest and it was agreed that they should be represented at the meeting by the two wingers Hugh Roberts and Frank Lindley

At the meeting, Roberts and Lindley were among the first five of the thirtyfive who stepped forward and volunteered to enlist. On reporting back to Luton, six more players travelled to London to sign up, defenders John Dunn, Robert Frith and T T Wilson and forwards Arthur Wileman, Arthur Roe and Ernest Simms. It is possible that their decision may have been influenced by the fact that they would receive army pay in addition to their club wages and would be granted leave every Saturday during army training to play football for their club. Other players and former players either joined the Football Battalion later or signed up to other Regiments direct and a number would never return home. League football was discontinued at the end of the season for the duration of the war.

1915-1919

Killed In Action

Pte.Thomas Clifford Royal Scots Fusiliers
Scottish defender with 31 appearances for Luton 1900-01. Killed on the Somme 19th January 1917 aged 42.

Lt. Ernest J Dodd Royal Field Artillery
Winger 1913-14. Killed in action 17th July 1917.

Pte. Frank Gilder London Regiment
Luton born amateur with no first team appearances. Sent to France March 1915 and killed in action at Loos on 30th December 1915.

Pte. Julius Gregory Royal Fusiliers
Played 42 games at full back for Luton in season 1908-09. An old boy of Manchester Grammar School he was killed at High Wood on the Western Front on 20th July 1916 aged 35.

Pte. John 'Jock' Jarvie 2nd Argyll & Sutherland Highlanders
Scottish full-back played 41 times for Luton between 1912 when he signed from Tottenham and 1914. He returned home to Glasgow at the end of season 1913-14 and enlisted straight away. He was one of fourteen men blown up by a mine. He was initially listed as 'missing' as his body could not be identified.

Pte. George Porter   Duke of Cambridge's Own Middlesex Regiment
Played just one game on the wing for Luton in season 1909-10. Killed in action on 14th July 1918 at Esquelbeoq.

Sgt. Arthur H Wileman M.M. Royal Sussex Regiment
Scored 58 goals in 107 appearances from 1912-15 and was one of the original eight Luton players to sign up for the 'Football' Battalion. Sent to France in 1916 he rose through the ranks to Sergeant and was awarded the Military Medal for bravery in the field in January 1918. He was killed on 28th April 1918 at Voormezeele, Flanders.

1915-1919

Wounded, Died, Etc.

Sgt. Thomas C Allsopp 18th Labour Battalion
Made 64 appearances on the wing for Luton between 1902-04 and also played cricket for Leicestershire and MCC from 1903-05 and Norfolk 1909-12. He purchased the Hero of Redan Pub in Norwich in 1911 but still enlisted in the Army Labour Corps. He survived the war but died in March 1919 in the influenza pandemic and was buried with full military honours.

Pte. Robert 'Walter' Fairgrieve 15th Battalion Royal Scots (Lothian Regiment)
Scottish centre-forward played 19 times for Luton in season 1899-1900. Enlisted in 1914 but did not see active service. Died in Edinburgh following an angina attack 2nd June 1915.

Pte. Westby Heath Royal Army Medical Corps
Played just seven games for Luton in 1914-15 and was one of the original eight to join the 'Football' Battalion. He transferred to the Medical Corps and was listed as 'wounded'. After the war he played for Stockport County and Chester.

Pte. Sydney Hoar Royal Field Artillery
Played 244 games on the wing for Luton before and after the war transferring to Arsenal in 1924. He joined the Bedfordshire Regiment in November 1916 but was discharged due to sickness in June 1916. He re-enlisted in September that year joining the Royal Field Artillery and was sent to France in June 1917. In August 1917 he was gassed and his football career put in doubt. He was sent home but returned to France in November 1917 and was demobilised two years later.

Pte. Frank Lindley 2nd Battalion Duke of Cambridge's Own Middlesex Regiment
One of the first two Luton players to enlist played just 5 games as a forward in 1914-15. He was sent to France in November 1915 and in August 1916 received a gunshot would to his left arm and was hospitalized in Belfast. He was sent back to France in March 1917 but invalided home suffering from impetigo in July 1917. Transferred to the Army Reserve in early 1919, he did not play again.

Pte. Hugh Roberts 17th (Service) Battalion Royal Middlesex Regiment
Joined Luton from Scunthorpe & Lindsey United for season 1914-15 and played all 42 games. He was one of the two Luton players first to enlist and was sent to France in 1915. He survived unscathed until sustaining a fractured ankle in an accident in September 1918 which ended his football career.

L.Cpl Arthur Roe 17th (Service) Battalion Middlesex Regiment

Played 138 times in the forward line for Luton both before and after the war. In 1925 he moved to Arsenal and then Bournemouth & Boscombe. According to some sources he was listed as 'wounded' but no details are available.

Pte. Ernest Simms 23rd (Service) Middlesex Battalion

A prolific goalscorer in 189 appearances for Luton before, during and after the war when he also became an England international. He was one of the original eight Luton players to enlist but seemed to think that football was more important than the war and on at least one occasion when released on leave to play for Luton didn't bother to go back to his unit until arrested by the police. Three times he was charged with being absent without leave and was admonished for the first offence but for the second and third was sentenced to Field Punishment Number 2 which involved hard labour while wearing leg shackles.

On 16th May 1916 he was convicted of desertion and had all his previous service from December 1914 forfeited. He was re-enlisted and in November 1917 was sent to Italy where on 18th April 1918 he was wounded receiving a gunshot wound to the right thigh. He was invalided home and discharged from hospital in February 1919. Sometime later the caretaker at Kenilworth Road discovered footprints in the snow on the cinder track around the pitch and on the terracing. Fearing attempted burglary, he alerted the police who set a trap and the following night caught Ernie Simms.

It transpired that since getting out of hospital he had been gaining access to the ground by climbing a drainpipe, stripping to his vest and pants and running to try to regain some fitness despite still having a severe limp and a very strange running gait. Luton directors took pity, didn't press charges and signed him for the 1919-20 season. The rest, as they say, is history.

Also Served

Pte. James Brandham (Regiment unknown)
Played just four games for Luton in the first season after the war. Is listed in the Luton Town FC Handbook 1919-20 as having served.

Pte. John Dunne 27th (Reserve) Middlesex Battalion
Full-back Dunne was another of the original eight Luton players to enlist,. He was transferred to the Reserve Battalion and then released to undertake essential munitions work in Liverpool. He played for Everton in wartime friendlies and returned to Luton in 1919 to complete 70 appearances.

Pte. Robert W Frith 27th (Reserve) Middlesex Battalion
Another of the original eight, Frith played 80 times in central defence for Luton. Before football he had been a furnaceman in Sheffield and he too was released for essential munitions work at a steel works in that city. He did not return to football after the war and according to some reports was living in distressed circumstances.

Pte Fred Hawkes (Regiment unknown)
Is listed in the Luton Town FC Handbook 1919-20 as having served. Came back after the war for just 14 games before retiring with a record breaking 625 appearances over more than twenty years.

Alexander McDonald (Royal Fleet Auxilliary)
Alex McDonald, an attacking midfielder, made 68 appearances and scored 16 goals for Luton in two spells between 1905 and 1911 before retiring. Ironically, having survived the war serving in the Royal Fleet Auxilliary he died by drowning in 1949 aged 71.

Pte. T T (Thomas?) Wilson   17th (Service Battalion) Middlesex Regiment
Defender T T Wilson played 67 times for Luton up to the outbreak of war and is the last of the original eight to sign up. No service record has been traced but it appears that he survived the war but did not return to football.

SEASON 1919-20

Only eight pre-war Luton players were in the season's squad. No less than 34 players were used and of these 26 were making their debut. Of these debutants, five played only one game, four played only two and five more played between three and five times. Three of the eight 'returners' were in the twilight of their careers, goalkeeper Harry Abbott played only four games mid-season, Bob Hawkes played just one game, the last of his 410 for the club on 26th April 1920.

Fred Hawkes played 14 games and bowed out on a record breaking 625 appearances on 1st May, the last game of the season in front of his home crowd. With such an unsettled team it was hardly surprising that the only two wins of note were 4-1 at Northampton and 4-0 at home to Newport County. There were a string of heavy defeats 4-0 at home to Merthyr Town, 4-0 away at Queens Park Rangers, 4-1 both home and away to Crystal Palace and 4-3 at Brighton, 4-2 at Watford and 5-0 at Bristol Rovers. The end result was 20th out of 22 narrowly avoiding relegation by one point.

Among the many debutants there were only three of particular note, Louis Bookman (aka Louis Buchalter) was an Irishman of Jewish/Lithuanian descent, who would appear 110 times and win three of his four Irish caps before leaving for Port Vale in 1923. He also played cricket as an all-rounder for Bedfordshire and Ireland where one of his international matches was against the West Indies. Allan Mathieson, another Irish inside forward, would play 58 times for Town winning his two Irish caps during this time. Mathieson was large for those days, described as 5'11" and 'wide', he moved on to other clubs including South Shields where he played over 100 games before emigrating and playing in both USA and Canada. Another inside forward, Harry Hickingbotham would score 39 goals in 99 appearances. In the FA Cup there was an away victory 1-0 at Brighton & Hove Albion and another 1-0 at Coventry City in a replay after 2-2 at Kenilworth Road. Defeat came in the 2nd Round 2-0 at home to Liverpool. On 30th May, it was announced that in the following season the Southern League Division 1 would form a new Division 3 of the Football League.

SEASON 1920-21

So the Hatters were back in the Football League if not by their own efforts and perhaps to celebrate, a new strip was ordered, the white shirt and black shorts that would be associated with them for over fifty years to come. This time only 19 players made their debut and only seven of these played five or less games. Among the rest were some who would have a significant influence.Goalkeeper Harry Bailey came in from Millwall as first choice to replace no less than four goalies used in the previous season. Bailey turned out 89 times for Luton before departing to Exeter City where he made over 150 appearances. Inside forward George Butcher, born in St Albans and once amateur lightweight boxing champion of Hertfordshire had played almost 100 league games for West Ham United and would make 129 appearances for Luton. George Lennon signed from Ayr United would make 115 appearances at full-back in his three seasons at Kenilworth Road and half-back William Molyneux came in from Liverpool and would turn out 85 times in two seasons.

Another signing from West Ham was full-back Alf Tirrell who would wear the white shirt 130 times. Two half-backs who each played only one game this season would nevertheless play many more in the future were Robert 'Bob' Millar (213) and Jimmy Walker (138).

With all this strengthening of defence it must have been a shock to travel to Swindon Town for the first game of the season to be beaten 9-1. Further defeats followed 4-1 at QPR, 4-1 at Merthyr Town and 5-0 to Bristol Rovers but things were turned round and some good wins followed at Kenilworth Road against Norwich 4-0, Gillingham 5-0, Reading 6-0 and Southend 4-0 leaving Luton in a respectable 9th place at the end of the season. Ernie Simms, back to full fitness was top scorer with 34 goals in 44 league and cup games. The FA Cup run broke two records. There was a 3-1 win at Rotherham County, a 2-1 home victory against Brimingham and a 4-0 victory at South Shields to put Luton into the 3rd Round for the first time in their history. They lost 3-2 to Preston North End watched by a new record Kenilworth Road crowd of 17,754.

SEASON 1921-22

Northern clubs had not been happy and felt hard done by when the Southern League became Football League Division 3 so it was decided that the league would now be called Division 3 (South) with a new Division 3 (North) being formed. In future years there were occasional switches between the two leagues to maintain the north/south balance. Luton now had a much more settled team with only 20 players being used throughout the season. There were good home wins 4-0 against Newport County, 4-0 versus Exeter and Gillingham were thrashed 7-0. Only once in the league did Town concede more than two goals, unfortunately 4-1 at Watford. There were just five new signings and two of these were significant, Robert 'Bob' Graham played only two games at full-back but would make 175 appearances in that position in the future.

Welshman Syd Reid was signed from his home town club Troed-y-rhiw Star and took over from Ernie Simms at centre forward in ten games at the end of the season. He would go on to score 81 goals in 143 matches up to his retirement in 1928. He would doubtless have scored many more had he not been too often plagued with injury.

Despite missing those later games Ernie Simms was still top scorer with 18 from 28 appearances, He was rewarded with a call-up to the England team to play Ireland on 22nd October 1921 becoming the first Third Division centre-forward to be chosen. His opponents included Allan Mathieson and Louis Bookman giving Luton three players on the pitch in a full international for the first time. The result was a 1-1 draw. In the FA Cup Portsmouth were beaten 2-1 in a replay at Kenilworth Road but there was defeat in the next round 1-0 at Aston Villa. Off the pitch, on 11th March 1922 a mysterious fire burned down the main stand at Kenilworth Road.

SEASON 1922-23

The first game of the season saw the official opening of the new main stand which was palatial compared to the one that had burned down which had presumably been well insured. Occupants of the new edifice witnessed a 2-2 draw with Charlton Athletic. Better home performances were to come with wins that included Brentford 4-0, Aberdare Athletic 4-1, Swansea Town 6-1, Exeter City 6-0 and Norwich City 4-0. Ernie Simms had left for South Shields and Syd Reid stepped up as top scorer with 18 goals from 33 appearances. The only major set-backs were away defeats 4-0 at both Plymouth Argyle and Queens Park Rangers. At the end of the season Luton were 5th behind champions Bristol City.

Thirteen players made their debut but five of these played three or fewer games and of the rest only three would play more than one season. The most important would be centre-half Bill Jennings signed from Merthyr Town who would go on to make 117 appearances in defence and captain the club. Only one game was played in the FA Cup, a 1-0 defeat away to Bury.

SEASON 1923-24

Another steady season with a 7th place finish in the Third Division (South). Town's best and worst performances were reserved for seaside towns with home wins against Portsmouth 4-1, Bournemouth 6-2, a home draw 4-4 with Southend United and a defeat 4-0 at Brighton. Syd Reid was injured for much of the season and Andy Kerr was brought in as his replacement at centre forward, top scoring with 20 goals from 39 starts. Reid netted six in the 13 games he started.

There were nine new signings including Kerr, three of which were 'one match wonders' but Stoke born Joe Till was signed from St Mirren and would make 144 appearances at full-back for Luton.There was a First Round exit again in the FA Cup with a 4-1 defeat against Arsenal at Highbury

SEASON 1924-25

Not such a good season with 6-0 against Merthyr Town and 4-0 versus Southend being the only really good home wins. Away form was dire with a 4-0 defeat at Plymouth, 4-1 defeats at Swindon, Swansea and Gillingham and only one away win all season.

Accordingly, Luton dropped to 16th place out of 22. Thirteen players made debuts but only one would feature in coming seasons, forward George Dennis who joint top scored with Syd Reid on 12 goals and would appear 150 times for Luton scoring 44 goals. Three of the thirteen newcomers are worth a mention, if only for their names. The three played only 25 games between them in this season and all moved on at season's end. The first two both went on to make over 150 league appearances for other clubs and the third had previously played for Clapton Orient and Northamton Town. The trio were Reg Tricker, Billy Thirlaway and Ernie Cockle – they don't name players like that anymore.

On 16th February 1925, Town appointed their first ever manager, George Thompson. Thompson was born in South Shields and played on the wing for Sheffield United and Derby County over 80 times in the seasons 1906-10. He was at Newcastle United in 1910-11 but didn't get a game. It appears that the Kenilworth Road job was his one and only foray into management. He lasted just eight months and Luton decided to do without such a luxury for another two years or so. Once again Town fell at the first hurdle in the FA Cup losing 4-0 to West Bromwich Albion at The Hawthorns.

SEASON 1925-26

The season started well and home wins were achieved against Bournemouth 4-1 and Newport County 4-2 and a 5-2 victory away at Aberdare. It was immediately after this win that manager George Thompson was sacked so his departure was apparently nothing to do with results.

After he had gone, the home form continued to be good with four goals scored against Merthyr, QPR, Swindon, Brentford and Bristol City. Gillingham were beaten 5-3 and best of all, Watford were seen off 5-0 at Kenilworth Road. Newcomer from Clapton Orient, J W 'Jimmy' Thompson top scored with 25 and George Dennis scored 15 as Luton eased their way back up to 7th place. There was also improvement in the FA Cup with a 3-1 home win against Folkestone before losing by the only goal at Aberdare Athletic in Round 2.

Of the 23 players used, 12 were playing for Luton for the first time but only three warrant notice, Jimmy Thompson already mentioned, would play another season before moving to Chelsea after scoring 42 goals in 74 starts. Wolverhampton born defender David Richards came in from Dundee and would make 152 appearances before leaving for Watford in 1931. The third is a true Luton legend, Scotsman Andy Rennie. As a youth player he was a goal scorer but his first club Kilwinning Rangers played him as a defender and Luton signed him as such He played his first two seasons at Kenilworth Road at centre-half and only started to be used up front in 1927-28 and it was the following season before he became a regular at centre-forward. Despite this late start, Rennie, known as 'Ratty' because of his short temper, would become Luton's second highest goal scorer of all-time with 162 goals from 355 appearances up to 1934. He had one season at Newport County after this but only played three games for them before retiring. He died in his late thirties in 1938 from complications following a hernia operation.

SEASON 1926-27

Just one place lower at 8th was this season's end result with some good home wins against Newport County 4-1, Coventry 4-1, Brighton 4-0 and Bournemouth 4-0. Bristol City won 6-0 on their home ground and Coventry reversed the score at home winning 4-1 but the strangest pair of results was over Christmas. On Christmas Day Luton beat Millwall 6-0 at Kenilworth Road and two days later at The Den, they fielded exactly the same team and were beaten 7-0, some turn-around. Joint top scorers were Syd Reid and Jimmy Thompson with 17 each. In the FA Cup Town reached the 3rd Round for the second time with two home wins against London Caledonians 4-2 and Northfleet United 6-2 but went out 4-0 at Stamford Bridge in their first ever meeting with Chelsea.

Once again the number of new players used was in double figures but this time no less than five of the eleven would feature for a number of seasons to come. Scottish wing-half John Black was signed from Chesterfield and would make 101 appearances before leaving for Bristol Rovers in 1930. Black lived to the ripe old age of 93 and his brother Adam holds the record for the most first team appearances for Leicester City. Midfielder Harry Woods came in from Arsenal having already played 330 league games for various clubs including 151 at Norwich. He would make 105 appearances for Luton scoring 27 goals. Another Scot forward Jimmy Yardley was signed from Clapton Orient and he would score 94 goals in 188 games before he was sold to Charlton Athletic in 1932. Londoner Charles Fraser would spend his entire professional career at Kenilworth Road playing in defence 272 times before retiring in 1935.

Harpenden born Henry Kingham another defender was signed from St Albans City and made 275 appearances before moving to Yeovil & Petters United in 1937 (name changed to Yeovil Town in 1946).

SEASON 1927-28

Not long after the start of the season on 14th September 1927, John McCartney was appointed as manager and became the first in a long line of Luton managers who had previously played for the club. On eight occasions Luton scored four or more when winning, the best being 6-1 against Crystal Palace and the same score versus Gillingham who were also beaten 4-0 away. Unfortunately Town conceded four or more in defeat in nine matches, the worst being 7-2 at Newport County. Probably the most bizarre was on Boxing Day when the game at Nothampton Town was played in a raging blizzard. Luton were 5-1 up at half-time but after a second half against the wind they lost 6-5. Joint top scorers in the league were Andy Rennie with 23 from 36 starts and Jimmy Yardley with 23 from 39 (plus 5 more from 3 cup games) but there were just too many defeats and Luton slipped to 13th place.

Once again there were a dozen debutants but none would have any great effect on the club's history. One though was interesting, the wonderfully named Septimus Randolph Galloway (always known as Randolph) played just 2 games and scored once for Luton but went on to manage seven clubs in Spain and Portugal including Sporting Gijon, Valencia CF, Real Racing Santander and Sporting Lisbon between 1929 and 1955 as well as a spell managing the national team of Costa Rica.

The 3rd Round was reached again in the FA Cup with fantastic home wins 9-0 against Clapton Orient and 6-0 versus Norwich City before defeat 2-1 at Burnden Park to Bolton Wanderers.

SEASON 1928-29

Scoring goals was still no problem at all but the defence had been tightened up which allowed Luton to move up to 7th place. Four or more goals were only conceded on four occasions and wins scoring four or more totalled nine with the best being 8-0 against Gillingham at Kenilworth Road when Andy Rennie netted five. Rennie was in his first full season at centre-forward as in the previous season he had played 15 of his 39 matches at centre-half and still scored 23 times. This season he netted 43 goals in 41 league games and also scored five goals in five cup ties. There were eleven new players used but none played any prominent part in the future and only four played more than one season.

The FA Cup saw Luton get to the 3rd Round once more. There was a 5-1 win against Southend United at Kenilworth Road with Andy Rennie getting four of them. Then there was a 0-0 draw at Craven Cottage before Luton won the replay 4-1. A home tie against Crystal Palace resulted in another 0-0 but in the replay at Selhurst Park the Hatters were dumped out 7-0.

SEASON 1929-30

In only five home games were four or more goals scored by Town, the best being 5-2 against Plymouth and the most satisfying 4-0 versus Watford. Away form was not good with 6-1 defeats at Plymouth and Clapton Orient, 5-1 at Bournemouth and Coventry and 4-1 at three other games. As a result Luton slipped back down the table to 13th. Andy Rennie was out due to injury mid-season and scored 17 from 27 games, Jimmy Yardley also scored 17 but from 41 starts and new signing from Brentford, Jimmy McKay Drinnan got 12 in his only season at the club. Other than Drinnan, among the new signings and worth a mention is goalkeeper George Harford. Harford signed from Millwall, would keep goal 107 times and as far as can be ascertained is no relation to the other two Harfords more famously associated with the club.

Also among the new signings was Albert Hutchinson. Hutchinson had come to Luton's notice scoring an incredible 255 goals in three seasons as an amateur for Sheffield club All Saints Old Boys. He played only five times and was sold to Torquay United at the end of the season. At Torquay he would make 338 appearances scoring 80 goals and appearing in every position for the club and as stand-in for an injured goalkeeper he even saved a penalty.

On 31st December manager John McCartney resigned citing ill health and was replaced the following day by coach George Kay being promoted from within. Kay had played 237 league games for West Ham United and was their captain at the first ever Wembley Cup Final, the famous 'White Horse' final.

After leaving Luton he would manage Southampton and then Liverpool from 1936 to 1951 winning the Division 1 title in 1947. There was to be no FA Cup run for Luton this year with a 3-2 defeat at Kenilworth Road to Queens Park Rangers in Round 1

SEASON 1930-31

An amazing fifteen players made their Luton debut with five playing less than five games and only four staying more than one season. Just two of these are worth a mention both Scottish, Hugh McGinnigle would appear 177 times in central defence and forward George McNestry who transferred from Sunderland. McNestry would score 29 goals in 79 games before moving to Bristol Rovers where he made over 100 league appearances. Top scorers were Andy Rennie with 20 and McNestry with 17. There were just three heavy away defeats 5-1 at Crystal Palace and Bristol Rovers and 4-0 at Gillingham but these were more than offset by eight home wins where Luton scored four or more the best being 5-0 against Fulham, 5-1 versus QPR and an 8-0 demolition of Thames Association. Final league position was an improved 7th and in the FA Cup Town drew 2-2 with Clapton Orient but won the replay, which was played at Highbury, 4-2. Unfortunately defeat came in the 2nd Round 3-1 at Vicarage Road, Watford.

When Luton played Thames Association on 6th December 1930 at their East London ground, a record was set which I understand still stands today, the lowest ever attendance at a Football League match. Just 469 spectators paid to see Luton lose 1-0.

I assume that there were very few away supporters among the 6,029 at Kenilworth Road for the reverse fixture when Luton scored eight. Thames were a short-lived team formed by a group of businessmen to play at an existing stadium in the West Ham area that was only being used for athletics and greyhound racing. Little support was forthcoming and they folded after a couple of seasons.

In May 1931, after the season had ended, Southampton enticed manager George Kay away and on 1st June, Harold Wightman was appointed to take his place. Wightman was a former centre-half with Chesterfield and Derby County and this was his first job in management. He stayed until 1935 and later managed both Mansfield Town and Nottingham Forest.

SEASON 1931-32

Once again goals were not a problem and Luton put six past Exeter and Reading and the last seven games of the season included home wins against Norwich City 7-1, Torquay United 6-1 and Swindon Town 6-0. Four goals or more in a defeat were conceded only three times and a steady 6th place in the league was achieved.Top scorers were newcomer Tommy Tait with 27 and Andy Rennie with 18. Tait was signed from Bolton Wanderers and would score an impressive 57 goals from 96 games before leaving for Bournemouth & Boscombe Athletic. He wasn't there long before another move to Reading where supporters contributed £200 towards the transfer fee. They were rewarded by him with a hat-trick in his first game and a total of 79 goals in 144 starts

Among the other signings was defender Fred Kean also from Bolton who had turned out 80 times for them and previously 230 times for Sheffield Wednesday and in the process won nine England caps, one as captain. He would further extend his career with 131 appearances for Luton. Jim Imrie came from Crystal Palace and would be first choice goalkeeper for the next couple of seasons and another worth a mention is Doug Rowe. Rowe was signed from a village team in Nottinghamshire and was only at Kenilworth Road for two seasons before moving to Lincoln. In addition to his skills as a left winger he was also English Amateur Champion wrestler at welterweight and also won prizes for weightlifting. His brother Bernard wrestled for Britain in the 1924 and 1928 Olympic Games and won a silver medal at the 1934 British Empire Games. Back on the football pitch, Luton reached the 3rd Round of the FA Cup again beating Swindon 5-0 away, drawing 2-2 at Lincoln City and winning the replay 4-1 at home before going out 2-1 to Wolverhampton Wanderers also at Kenilworth Road.

SEASON 1932-33

Luton slipped to 14th in the table but on the plus side reached the quarter-finals of the FA Cup for the first time. Despite the lower position, there were some interesting games for the home fans with Tommy Tait scoring a hat-trick in both the 8-1 mauling of Cardiff City and the 5-5 draw with Brentford. Andy Rennie got three in each of the wins against Bristol City 5-4 and Swindon Town   6-2. There were two signings of note, County Durham born Tom Mackey came in from Sheffield Wednesday and would play 208 games in Luton's defence up to his retirement in 1938.

47

Centre-half Albert Hayhurst played just two games for Town but would make 237 league appeances for Reading. He also played first-class cricket for Warwickshire as a fast-medium bowler in 1934-5 and was still playing minor counties cricket for Buckinghamshire in 1953 at the age of 48.

The record FA Cup run started with a 2-2 draw at Kenilworth Road against Kingstonian. The replay at Kingston-upon-Thames was won 3-2 and there was a win by the same score away to Stockport County. In the next round there was another home draw 0-0 with Barnsley followed by a 2-0 win at Oakwell. In the 4th Round Luton actually managed a home win beating Tottenham Hotspur 2-0 and the same score was enough to account for Halifax Town away at The Shay. The dream came to an end at Goodison Park in the 6th Round when Everton won 6-0 in what was the first ever meeting between the two sides.

SEASON 1933-34

Town bounced back to 6th place with the highlights being 4-2 home wins against Gillingham and QPR, a 4-0 away win at Cardiff City and the best, 10-2 against Torquay United at Kenilworth Road with evergreen Andy Rennie netting four. Rennie was the club's top scorer again with newcomer Tommy Bell scoring 14. His namesake Sam Bell scored two in the single game he played and would contribute well in the following season

A new competition was launched, the Division Three (South) Cup. Luton were drawn away to Aldershot and lost 4-3. In the FA Cup, much was expected after the previous season's exploits but the 1st Round draw brought the mighty Arsenal to Kenilworth Road.

The Gunners won by the only goal of the match but there was consolation for the Board, if not the fans, as a new attendance record of 18,626 was set.

SEASON 1934-35

Luton equalled their best finish in Div 3(S) at 4th scoring four or more goals in ten of their wins, the best being 6-1 against Aldershot and 6-2 versus Bristol Rovers. A Christmas Day 4-0 win against Brighton & Hove Albion was followed on Boxing Day by a 4-1 defeat at the Goldstone Ground in Hove and Torquay United got their revenge for the previous seasons thrashing by winning 6-2 at Plainmoor. Andy Rennie scored just one goal in twelve games in his last season. He moved to Newport County but played only three league games for them before retiring. Luton's new top scorer was Sam Bell with twentyone.

Among the fifteen players making their Hatters debut, five would be very significant. Tom Smith would appear 172 times in defence and goalkeeper Joe Coen, signed from Celtic would play between the sticks on 158 occasions. Forward George Stephenson would turn out 212 times and score 69 goals and Fred Roberts, signed from Birmingham City would make 198 appearances and score 45 goals staying with the club until 1945. A certain Joe Payne was signed from Bolsover Colliery, played just two games at left-half and showed no sign of what was to come in future years

Luton were drawn away twice in the Third Division (South) Cup winning at Gillingham but going out 2-1 at Queens Park Rangers. In the FA Cup, there was an excellent 1-1 draw at Stamford Bridge and 23,041 (another record) crammed themselves into Kenilworth Road to see a 2-0 replay win. In Round 4 there was another away tie at Burnley and Luton lost 3-1.

SEASON 1935-36

An excellent season and 2nd place but no promotion as only one each from Divisions 3(S) and 3(N) were promoted. Among the new signings were a half-back trio that would be virtually ever-present in the 1936-37 season and vital to the future. Jock Finlayson would make 168 appearances, Jack Nelson 148 and Bill Fellowes, signed from Clapton Orient 124 before his departure to Exeter City in 1938. Top scorer was George Stephenson with 14 and there were some good home wins against Crystal Palace 6-0, Clapton Orient 5-3, Newport County 7-0 and the one everyone remembers Bristol Rovers 12-0 on Easter Monday 13th April when Joe Payne was credited with TEN goals – a league record which still stands. Payne had played just four games at right-half at the beginning of the season and then, surplus to requirements, he was loaned out to Biggleswade Town. Due to several injuries he was brought back and on the day with both centre-forwards out, he was asked to wear the number 9 shirt. My mother and father were there in their courting days on a cold wet afternoon.

They always maintained that he only scored nine and that his last was only scored when he was sitting on his backside in the mud and the ball was passed to his out-stretched boot by a player who could have walked it into the net. My parent's claim of 'only nine' could be explained by the fact that one goal was given to him after the match by the referee who ruled that the ball had crossed the line before the player who Mum & Dad thought to have scored had touched it.

Either way, it's in the book as ten and the most annoyed must have been Bob Bell who had scored nine for Tranmere Rovers in their 13-4 win over Oldham Athletic only a few months before on Boxing Day 1935 and would have thought that his record would stand for a long time. Payne would score 83 goals in 72 appearances and win his only England cap before being sold to Chelsea in 1938 for £2,000. On April 25th the attendance record was broken again with 23,559 watching a 1-1 draw with champions to be Coventry City. Had Luton won they would have been promoted. In the 3rd Division (South) Cup, despite George Stephenson rocketing a hat-trick, what was virtually a reserve Luton side went out 5-3 at Swindon. The FA Cup saw a 2-2 draw at West Ham followed by a 4-0 victory in the replay but a loss in Round 4 to Manchester City 2-1 at Maine Road.

SEASON 1936-37

Champions! Edward 'Ned' Liddell had taken over as manager on 13th August 1936 and steered Luton to first place and promotion. Born in County Durham, Liddell had played 193 league games at half-back for Clapton Orient and had previously managed Queens Park Rangers and Fulham. Liddell had a settled team all season with inside-forward Fred Roberts and left-back Tom Smith playing all 42 league games. There were only four games when one of the half-back trio of Jock Finlayson, Jack Nelson and Bill Fellowes was missing. Left-winger George Stephenson played 37 games and 'Ten Goal' Joe Payne 39, in those 39 he scored a record 55 goals with three more in four cup games. (The outright record is held by Dixie Dean 60 goals in 39 matches for Everton in 1927-28).

The number of new players used was the lowest for a number of years and only two made much of a contribution to the succesful campaign. A G 'Bert' Dawes had scored 178 goals in 289 matches for Northampton and Crystal Palace and in this season netted eight in 21 games at inside-forward and winger Ted Hancock who had made over 100 appearances for Burnley, played 18 times and scored once. One newcomer who played only a handfull of games but is worth a mention is J E 'Eddie' Parris. Parris, born near Chepstow, had played 142 times for Bradford Park Avenue and in 1931 had become the first black player to represent Wales. His white mother and father of Jamaican descent were both born in Canada.

In the league season there were twelve wins when Luton scored four or more, the best being 8-1 against Cardiff City with Joe Payne scoring four. In the last six games of the season there were wins versus Gillingham 5-2 (Payne 4), Aldershot 5-2 (Payne 2), Swindon 5-1 (Payne 3) and Newport County 5-0 (Payne 3). Despite this, Luton still needed to win the last game of the season against Torquay United to clinch the title and 20,755 turned up at Kenilworth Road to see them do it 2-0 (Payne 2) – Not bad for a converted half-back. In the FA Cup there was a 3-3 home draw with Blackpool followed by a 2-1 replay win at Bloomfield Road and another home draw 2-2 against Sunderland but this time there was defeat in the replay 3-1. What was basically a reserve team competed in the Div 3(South) Cup but still had wins against Bournemouth and Aldershot before defeat 4-2 against Notts County. A team photograph with the championship shield shows Luton in a new strip, still black shorts and white shirts but with a large badge on the shirt on which the Hatters straw boater is prominent for the first time. Another photograph proves that a crowd surging onto a pitch after winning the league is nothing new

SEASON 1937-38

Ready for the first season back in Division 2 for 37 years, both the main stand and the Kenilworth Road terracing were extended allowing a new attendance record to be set when 25,349 saw Aston Villa beaten 3-2 in the first home game of the season on 1st September. The record was broken again when 25,746 attended a 2-1 win in an FA Cup tie against Swindon Town on 22nd January 1938.

Goals still came fairly easily with the best performances being away at Southampton 6-3 and Swansea Town 5-1 with a 6-4 home win against Stockport County. On eight other occasions Luton netted four goals. Joe Payne wasn't so prolific with 16 goals from 23 games. Fred Roberts scored 12 from 37 and newcomer E J 'Jack' Vinall netted 15 from 33 games in league and cup. A respectable 12th was the final league position. On 26th February 1938, Ned Liddell resigned to become Head Coach at Chelsea and it was probably no coincidence that Joe Payne was sold to Chelsea about a fortnight later for £2,000. Luton managed without a manager for the rest of the season. Joe Payne remains Luton's best ever goal scorer in terms of goals per game at 1.129. Even if you discount the ten goal game he is still better than one per game at 1.013. Nearest to him are Hugh Billington 0.745 and John O'Rourke on 0.733. (This is discounting Harry Loasby who achieved 0.933 but only played 15 games). To put these figures in context, some of Town's more prolific scorers rate as follows: Gordon Turner 0.613, Malcolm McDonald 0.574, Danny Hylton 0.555 and Andre Gray 0.513.

The number of new players used was back into double figures but only two are worthy of note, Jack Vinall had scored 80 goals in 181 appearances for Norwich City and is now in that club's Hall of Fame. He would score 20 in 50 games for Luton. Dumbarton born inside-forward Eddie Connelly came in from Newcastle United and would score 16 goals in 51 games before being sold to West Bromwich Albion in August 1939 just before league football was suspended due to WW2. After the war in 1946 he came back to Kenilworth Road and took his tally to 90 games and 24 goals. The new manager appointed in June 1938 was Neil McBain who had previously managed Watford and Ayr United.

He would stay with Luton for about a year. After the war he briefly managed two English clubs before going to Argentina to manage Estudiantes de La Plata from 1949-51. To date he remains the only British manager of Estudiantes. After this adventure he returned to Ayr, Watford and Ayr again before retiring.

SEASON 1938-39

More ground improvements had been made in the close season and fans at the Oak Road End had a roof over their heads for the first time. A steady season saw some good results and a 7th place finish. There were away wins at Bury 5-2 and Southampton 6-2 and home wins against Chesterfield 5-0, Nottingham Forest 4-2 and Swansea Town 6-3 when new boy Hugh Billington scored four. Billington, born in Ampthill but brought up in Luton, had been signed from Waterlows (A major printing works in nearby Dunstable) where he had scored no less than 80 goals in 1937-38. He did so well in the reserves that he replaced Jack Vinall at centre forward after 12 games and became top scorer in Division 2 with 28 goals from just 27 games. His career tally at Luton of 70 goals in 94 appearances would have been very much greater had he not lost seven seasons due to WW2. He was sold to Chelsea for £8,000 in 1948 and made 83 league starts for them. Town's other main scorers were Eddie Connelly and Billy Redfern with 13 each and the evergreen George Stephenson with twelve.

Other than Hugh Billington, only five players made their Luton debut the unluckiest of which must have been goalkeeper Sam Mayberry. Since 1935 goal-keeping duties had been shared between Bill Dolman and Joe Coen but Mayberry came in for the last game of the season against Coventry City at Kenilworth Road. He let in three, Luton lost and thanks to WW2, this was Mayberry's one and only game for the Hatters. In the FA Cup Luton came out of the hat to play Liverpool at Anfield and 40,341 watched them lose 3-0. In June manager Neil McBain resigned due to the ill health of his wife – he would not be replaced until 1944.

1939-1946

The history books will tell you that there was no league football in this period but in fact three games of the 1939-40 season were played before war-time restrictions put an end to league football. These games were expunged from official records but the facts are that Luton beat Sheffield Wednesday 3-0 and drew 1-1 with Fulham at Kenilworth Road and beat Bradford Park Avenue 3-0 away and when war was declared Luton with 5 points were top of the league above Birmingham City on goal average.

Unlike the First World War, I am able to find only one Luton player who gave his life in this conflict, goalkeeper Joe Coen. Coen was signed from Clydebank and made 158 appearances for Town, the last being on 29th April 1939. He was killed in an RAF training accident in 1941.

Competitive football resumed with the FA Cup in January 1946. Luton got no further than Round 3 losing 6-0 at home and 3-0 away in a two-legged tie against Derby County. This was the first and only time that the cup was played over home and away ties up to the semi-finals and was done to give much needed revenue to the clubs with league football not resuming until later in the year.

There were only two pre-war players in the Luton teams and it was no disgrace to lose to Derby as they went on to win the cup 4-1 in extra time against Charlton Athletic at Wembley.

By now Luton were managed by one of their former players Scotsman George Martin who had won the Division 1 title with Everton before playing over 100 games for the Hatters. He became a coach at Luton in 1939 and was made manager in December 1944.

SEASON 1946-47

Of the 26 players used in the season only two, Hugh Billington and Eddie Connelly had played for Luton pre-war. Among the newcomers, several would be of significance, Douglas 'Dally' Duncan a winger who had played over 250 games for Derby and won 14 Scottish caps would not play many matches but was a future Luton manager. Another winger Billy Waugh, known as 'The Rabbit' because of his speed, would make 147 appearances before leaving for QPR in 1950. Half-back Wally Shanks would play 276 times and defender Bill Cooke make 228 appearances in a Luton shirt. Goalkeeper Bernard Streten from Norfolk would play 299 times in the green jersey and wear a yellow one once when he won his only England cap. (In those days goalkeepers always wore green and only England keepers wore yellow).

Another player regularly in the team was Hong 'Frank' Soo who played for Stoke City pre-war and briefly for Leicester City before signing for Luton for a £5,000 fee. He was the first player of Chinese extraction (white mother, Chinese father) to play in the Football League and the first non-white player to represent England although these were war time internationals (on release from the RAF) and not full caps. Bernard Streten and Wally Shanks are the earliest Luton signings who I actually saw play.

The highlights of the season were wins 4-1 against Sheffield Wednesday and 6-3 versus Notts County in the last game of the season. In the game against high flying Newcastle United at Kenilworth Road, Luton were 3-0 down at half time but came back to win 4-3.

The attendance record was broken again on 16th November when 26,362 crammed into the ground to see Spurs beaten 3-2. Hugh Billington was the season's top scorer helping Luton to a mid-table 13th place finish. In the FA Cup the 5th Round was reached with home wins 6-0 over Notts County and 2-0 against Swansea Town. A third home tie saw a 0-0 draw with Burnley winning the replay 3-0.

SEASON 1947-48

Goals seemed harder to come by and the only Luton score over three was in the 6-1 home defeat of Leeds United on 27th December after a 2-0 win against them the previous day, the first time the teams had met competitively. There was no movement in league position which was again 13th. Off the pitch, George Martin had been enticed away by Newcastle in the close season and Dally Duncan was given the job of player-manager.

Also pre-season Luton had signed Welsh international full-back W M 'Billy' Hughes from Birmingham City for a record club fee of £11,000 but before the season was over he was sold to Chelsea along with high scoring Hugh Billington for a combined £20,000. Among the new signings were Bobby Brennan and W H 'Buster' Collins both imported from Irish football, a policy that would prove very successful over the coming years but the most important signing, also from Birmingham, was that of Syd Owen. A true Luton legend, Syd played initially at wing-half before becoming a permanent fixture as centre-half and captain making 423 appearances and winning three England caps. He skippered Luton at Wembley in 1959 before retiring and taking the hot seat as manager.

Tottenham Hotspur were the visitors once again responsible for the attendance record being taken to 26,496 in October when the record crowd were treated to a goal-less draw. As in the previous season, the 5th Round was reached in the FA Cup with a 4-2 win versus Plymouth Argyle at Home Park and a 3-2 win against Coventry City at Kenilworth Road before defeat 3-1 away to Queens Park Rangers.

SEASON 1948-49

There were only three high scoring games and two of those were against Lincoln City 6-0 at Kenilworth Road and 4-4 at Sincil Bank, the third being a 4-3 home win against Nottingham Forest. League position was up slightly at 10th. Top scorer was South African J W 'Willy' Arnison signed from Rangers for £8,000, with 19 goals from 32 games.

October 30th 1948 against West Ham saw the first team debut of another Luton legend. Aston Clinton born R H 'Bob' Morton like Hugh Billington had been spotted playing for Waterlows at Dunstable and was signed as an amateur in 1945, turning professional in 1946. He would go on to make a record 495 league appearances and 562 in all competitions playing in defence, in midfield and up-front scoring 55 goals.

Others to make their debut included full-back Tom 'Bud' Aherne who was signed from Belfast Celtic and who had previously played both football and hurling for Limerick. He would make 288 appearances for Luton and win 15 international caps for both N.Ireland and Ireland in his time at the club. Another double centurion was Scottish midfielder Charlie Watkins signed from Rangers, he would turn out 239 times. When his playing days were over, he bacame a coach at Kenilworth Road and was briefly caretaker manager in the 1960s. In the FA Cup there were home wins versus West Ham 3-1 and Walsall 4-0 followed by a very high scoring tie against Leicester in the 5th Round. A 5-5 draw at Kenilworth Road was followed by a replay win for the Foxes 5-3 at Filbert Street.

SEASON 1949-50

Luton dropped to 17th place with only ten wins and an amazing eighteen draws, half of which were goal-less. Five of those 0-0 scores were in six consecutive matches in March/April 1950 – not a good time to be a Hatters supporter. The only highlight was a 5-2 home win against Blackburn Rovers with newcomer George Stobbart netting four (He only scored five more but was the season's top scorer with just that nine).

This was more than offset by defeats 5-2 at Bury and 6-1 at Grimsby Town. Grimsby also put Luton out of the FA Cup winning 4-3 in the 3rd Round at Kenilworth Road. Despite this dire form there was yet another record attendance of 27,319 in October for the visit of Tottenham Hotspur. The result, you've guessed it, a draw 1-1.

George Stobbart, a former miner from Morpeth, had been signed from Newcastle United and would score 30 goals in 116 games for Luton before leaving for Millwall in 1952. The other signing of note was goalkeeper Iorwerth 'Lorrie' Hughes from Llandudno Town. He played only 36 times but won all four of his Welsh international caps while with the Hatters, the first against England in 1951. It was probably around this time that the Hatters started to be of interest to me as I remember christening a kitten 'Luton' because it was black and white and a number of players I would watch in future years were already in place at the club – Syd Owen, Bob Morton, Bernard Streten, Bud Aherne and Wally Shanks who would eventually be a coach at the club and half of Shanks & Turner Sports Outfitters.

SEASON 1950 -51

There were no fewer than fifteen goalscorers in the season but none netted more that nine times and Luton slipped even further down to 19th place with just nine wins all season. There were two bright spots at home with wins of 4-0 against Grimsby and 4-2 versus Bury but away form was very poor with losses including 4-1 at Bury, 5-2 at Doncaster Rovers, 5-3 at Hull City and 6-1 at Barnsley. FA Cup form was not much better with both ties at home Town beat Portsmouth 2-0 but lost 2-1 to Bristol Rovers in the 4th Round.

There were three debutants of note. Gordon Turner played just two games at right-half and didn't score which was something that couldn't be said for many seasons to come when he would be Lutons all-time top goal scorer and total legend with 276 goals from 450 appearances. Doncaster born Turner had been spotted playing in the Royal Navy during National Service and signed as an apprentice in 1949 no doubt helped by the fact that manager Dally Duncan had played alongside Gordon's father, also a professional footballer. Luton was Welsh full-back Les Jones's first club and he played 109 times before signing for Aston Villa.

Bernard Moore had played for Brighton but was released to Hastings after leaving the RAF in 1947 (apparently it was supposed to be a temporary loan but an administrative error made it a full transfer).Moore scored 138 goals in 121 games for Hastings and Luton paid £4,000 for him (a record for a Southern League player). Moore having scored 34 times in 85 games for the Hatters he was sold back to Brighton, his home town club, for £3,000. Later in his career Moore became a part of Bedfordshire folklore playing for Bedford Town in the FA Cup 3rd Round against the mighty Arsenal at Highbury in January 1956. Arsenal were 2-0 up at half time but the Eagles pulled one back and then Moore scored the goal which would mean a replay at The Eyrie. In the replay Bedford were 1-0 up for much of the game but Arsenal got an equalizer with four minutes to go and scored the winner in extra time. Bernard Moore was at the Kenilworth Road Centenary celebration in 2005 and lived to be ninety.

SEASON 1951-52

Luton achieved a much improved 8th place in the league and reached the quarter-finals of the FA Cup for only the second time High scoring games included home wins against Sheffield Wednesday 5-3, West Ham 6-1, Barnsley 4-2 and Notts County 6-0. County got their own back winning 5-4 at Meadow Lane as did Wednesday with a 4-0 score at Hillsborough.The cup run started with a 1-0 home win against Charlton Athletic but it then took three games to dispose of Brentford, 2-2 at home, 0-0 at Griffin Park and finally a 3-2 win in the 2nd replay staged at Highbury. Swindon Town were beaten 3-1 at Kenilworth Road which was also the venue for the 6th Round tie against Arsenal with the Gunners winning 3-2. Many in the new record crowd of 28,433 thought that Luton were very unlucky to lose. Top scorers in league and cup were Jack Taylor with 24 and Bert Mitchell on seventeen.

A number of important players made their first team debut. Seamus Dunne had been signed from Shelbourne in 1950 and would play 326 times at full-back winning 15 caps for the Republic of Ireland in his time at Luton. He later worked at Vauxhall Motors and was player-manager of Dunstable Town before returning to Ireland. South African Roy Davies was bought from Clyde and would score 28 goals from the wing in 169 appearances and another winger, Bert Mitchell from Northampton Town would score 43 goals in 119 appearances in his four seasons at the club. Yet another winger Scotsman Mike Cullen signed as a youth player in 1948 played just the last two games of the season. He became one of my favourites with 126 appearances and 19 goals, winning his only Scottish cap against Austria in 1956.

One player who made little impression in his one season before returning to West Ham would later become famous as manager of clubs including Chelsea and Manchester United and the England U21 side – Dave Sexton.

SEASON 1952-53

Before the season started, Skipper Syd Owen had the important task and great honour of autographing and presenting me with my certificate for 1st Place in the Boys House Relay at Houghton Regis Voluntary Primary School sports. This was a great improvement on my previous best of second place in Boys 75yds Skipping two years earlier. Luton also greatly improved coming 3rd behind Huddersfield Town and champions Sheffield United and only missing promotion by virtue of two draws and two losses in the last four games of the campaign.Good home wins included Blackburn Rovers and Barnsley both 6-0, Notts County 5-1 and four other scores of four. Top goalscorer was new signing Jesse Pye with 28 from 43 games and Gordon Turner was beginning to find the net with 16 from 23 appearances.

Jesse Pye had been signed for £5,000 from Wolverhampton Wanderers where he had scored 90 times in 188 league games and won his only England cap. He was sold to Derby in 1954 having taken his Luton goal tally to 36. He was only 33 when he came to Kenilworth Road but I remember his as looking ancient but he had seen war service in North Africa and Italy so perhaps that was the reason.

A much more significant debutant was goalkeeper Ron Baynham born in Birmingham and signed from Worcester City. Ron would become another Luton Legend appearing in goal 434 times and winning three England caps. The FA Cup saw progress to the 5th Round with a 6-1 win against Blackburn Rovers at Kenilworth Road where Manchester City were beaten 5-1 after a 1-1 draw at Maine Road. At home again, Town went out 1-0 to Bolton Wanderers.

SEASON 1953-54

The season opened with a 4-4 draw at Kenilworth Road with Oldham but if fans thought goals galore were to come they were disappointed as that was the most Luton scored all season. It came courtesy of a hat-trick from Scottish newcomer John Downie. Downie had a very long playing career starting at Bradford Park Avenue in 1942, playing 110 times for Manchester United, making just 26 appearances for Luton and ending his career at Stalybridge Celtic in 1962. Downie and Bert Mitchell both totalled 12 but top scorer for the first but by no means the last time was Gordon Turner with 16 helping Luton to a comfortable 6th place behind champions Leicester City. Three players who would play a big part in future seasons made their debut, half-back John Groves had signed as a youth player in 1949, turning professional on his 17th birthday. He would make 251 appearances for Town before being sold to Middlesborough in 1963. Inside-forward George Cummins was signed from Everton and would score 30 goals in 209 starts for Luton winning 19 caps for Republic of Ireland while at the club.

Scottish outside-left Jimmy Adam was signed from Spennymoor and made 144 appearances with 24 goals before being sold to Aston Villa. He later emigrated and played for a Melbourne team.

The 3rd Round of the FA Cup took four games to settle and got me into trouble. There was a 1-1 draw at Blackpool and when the replay was fixed for the following Wednesday afternoon, a mate and I decided that a bus to Kenilworth Road was a much better option than getting covered in cold January mud pretending to play rugby at Dunstable Grammar School games afternoon. We enjoyed a fairly entertaining game despite it being a 0-0 draw and were not particulary surprised when at assembly the following morning we were invited to attend the Headmaster's study. We both had fairly reasonable excuses ready until we saw his daily paper open on his desk with a photograph captioned, 'A section of the Luton crowd' and guess who front centre. We had no choice but to put our hands up and accept the punishment, (which he told us would be 'serious'), of writing a 500 word report on the match. On 7th October 1953, the first ever match under floodlights was played at Kenilworth Road

SEASON 1954-55

Promotion to the top flight of English football was achieved for the first time in the club's history. Luton won their last three games of the season at home to Port Vale 4-2 and Bristol Rovers 2-0 and crucially 3-0 away at Doncaster Rovers. This left three teams all on 54 points and decided on goal average it was Champions Birmingham City, 2nd and promoted Luton Town, 3rd and unlucky Rotherham United.

Goal Average was the number of goals scored divided by the number of goals conceded, it was replaced by goal difference in season 1978-79 to encourage more attacking play. Best results had been a 7-3 win against Blackburn Rovers at Kenilworth Road, away wins at Nottingham Forest 5-1 and Hull City 4-0 and a 4-4 draw at Anfield. Gordon Turner and full-backs Seamus Dunne and Bud Aherne were ever-present during the successful league campaign and half-back Wally Shanks only missed three even playing on the left wing in those last three vital games when Scotsmen Jimmy Adam and Mike Cullen were not available (Wally had made his debut on the wing in 1947). Bob Morton missed only four games playing at both right-half and centre-forward and contributing 14 goals. Ron Baynham and Bernard Streten played roughly half a season each in goal and the other main contributors were Roy Davies, Jim Pemberton, George Cummins and of course, skipper Syd Owen at centre-half. Gordon Turner top scored with 37 goals in league and cup.

Two players of note made first team debuts, utility player Terry Kelly had signed from Vauxhall Motors in 1950 and would go on to make 149 appearances mostly in defence. Reg Pearce came in from Winsford United in Cheshire and became one of my favourite players, never seeming to have a bad game at half-back. He played 83 times before being sold to Sunderland. In the FA Cup there was a 5-0 home win against Workington Town and then a 5-1 away at Rotherham United with a Turner hat-trick but Manchester City proved too strong at Kenilworth Road winning 2-0 in the 5th Round.

SEASON 1955-56

Luton's first ever goal in Division 1 was scored in a 2-2 draw with Charlton at The Valley by who else but Gordon Turner who would top score with 19 goals. Being in the top flight was certainly attracting the crowds and the November 1955 match against Wolves saw what is still the highest attendance for a league match at Kenilworth Road of 27,911 and the season average of 21,455 is still a record. Big scores were not so easy to come by and a 5-1 win at home in that match against Wolves and 4-0 away at Sheffield United were good results but the one I saw and will always remember was the 8-2 demolition of Sunderland who, when they arrived at Kenilworth Road were top of the table. Mick Cullen and Gordon Turner each netted twice with one for Jimmy Adam and a rare Bob Morton hat-trick completed the rout. Luton also won the return game and the Black Cats must have hated visiting Kenilworth Road as they were also hit with very high scores in the next two seasons. The final league position was 10th, not bad for a first season among the big boys but there was nothing to cheer about in the FA Cup with a 4-0 defeat at home to lowly Leicester City.

At this time Luton had three goalkeepers on their books who had or would represent England, Ron Baynham and Bernard Streten (full caps) and Alan Collier, a local boy from Markyate who was an England Youth international. All were kept busy in action for the First Team, Reserves or A Team, there was no sitting on a substitutes bench in those days. Two players of interest made their debut, George McLeod was signed from the Scottish Highland League, made 60 appearances between 1955-58 but would go on to make over 200 appearances for Brentford.

Forward Tony Gregory was picked up from Vauxhall Motors. He would only make 74 appearances for Luton but one of those would be in the FA Cup Final before he left for rivals Watford helping them to promotion in 1959-60.

SEASON 1956-57

In the close season the Oak Road End terracing was doubled in height and was a lot more comfortable as I stood there for the first game of the season to see Sunderland hammered once more, this time 6-2 with Gordon Turner scoring four. Two more wins followed and on 25th August 1956 Luton sat at the top of the Division 1 table for the first time ever. Obviously it couldn't last and 16th was the final result. Gordon Turner scored three more hat-tricks in the home wins against Charlton 4-2 and Newcastle 4-1 and also in the 5-4 defeat away to Wolverhampton. His final tally was 30 in the league plus 5 in cup matches and to put this in perspective, Lutons next highest scorer was Bob Morton with just five. There were however some nasty defeats, 4-0 at home to Chelsea and away at Blackpool 4-0, Tottenham 5-0 and West Bromwich Albion 4-0. The FA Cup saw a 3rd Round exit 2-0 in a replay at Aston Villa after a 2-2 draw at Kenilworth Road.

There was better luck in a new competition, the Southern Professional Floodlit Cup which Luton won at the first time of asking. At Kenilworth Road Chelsea were beaten 4-2 (another Turner hat-trick) and Watford 4-3 and in the semi-final away to Brentford there was a 4-0 win. In the final away at Reading, Town couldn't keep the four goal sequence going but won 2-1.

Two more FA Cup finalists to be made their debut, full back Brendan McNally had been signed from Shelbourne and would make 163 appearances and win three Republic of Ireland caps before leaving for Cambridge City and ending his career at Dunstable Town. Forward Allan Brown had won 14 Scottish caps and was signed from Blackpool for £8,000. He would score 58 goals in 175 games for Luton before leaving for Portsmouth in 1960 and would return to Kenilworth Road in 1966 as manager.

SEASON 1957-58

Despite a couple of nasty losses 5-0 at Portsmouth and 4-1 at Leicester, there were also some good wins at home including West Bromwich 5-1, Arsenal 4-0 and the by now traditional Sunderland 7-1 (Gordon Turner 4). Turner was again top scorer with 33 in the league and 5 in the cups. Why wasn't he playing for England? The reward was 8th place, the highest so far. The FA Cup was best forgotten with a cringeworthy 3-0 defeat away to 3rd Division(N) Stockport County (Who have the temerity to also call themselves the Hatters). In the catchily named Southern Professional Floodlit Cup Luton only reached the semi-final beating Southampton 2-0 at St Marys and Brentford 7-1 in a Kenilworth Road replay after a 0-0 result at Griffin Park. Reading were held 3-3 away but got their revenge for the previous season with a 1-0 win at Luton.

1957 was the last time Luton played a game on Christmas Day and it resulted in a 3-0 defeat at Old Trafford but there was cause to celebrate in that it marked the debut of Luton born Dave Pacey at half-back

72

He had been playing for Hitchin Town and was signed by Luton as soon as he completed his National Service. His early form was so impressive that Luton felt able to sell Reg Pearce to Sunderland for a large fee and Dave would play 280 times for Luton before leaving for Kettering in1965. The other significant debutant was full-back Ken Hawkes who was signed as a youth player from Shotton Colliery Welfare in 1951 and made 106 appearances before his transfer to Peterborough in 1961.

SEASON 1958-59

After a bright start Luton slipped to 17th in the league but nobody remembers that because this was the Wembley season. At the end of September after ten games unbeaten Luton were top of the table with those games including home wins against West Ham 4-1, Manchester City 5-1 and Preston 4-1. On Boxing Day Arsenal were beaten 6-3 and other wins included Burnley 6-2, Leicester 4-3, Newcastle 4-2 and Nottingham Forest 5-1 but there were too many losses especially away from home. Gordon Turner suffering from a number of injuries scored 16 goals from 34 games but top scorer was Allan Brown with 25. The semi-final was reached again in the Southern Floodlit Cup with Portsmouth beaten 2-0 away and Southampton 4-0 at home before defeat 1-0 by Crystal Palace at Selhurst Park. Before the season had started Billy Bingham had been signed from Sunderland where he had made 206 appearances. He would play exactly 100 times for Luton and score 33 goals from the wing before departing for Everton.

Bingham played 56 times for Northern Ireland (9 times while with the Hatters) and had two spells managing his country earning the MBE. He had earlier earned my sister's undying love, she tells me 'He used to smell nice' as he ran past.

Manager Dally Duncan had left for Blackburn Rovers in October so Luton were effectively without a manager for the whole of their best ever run in the FA Cup. Tony Gregory was controversially preferred to Jimmy Adam on the left wing and Gordon Turner had been struggling with injury but was fit for the latter stages. He was however left out and whoever was choosing the team stayed with the same eleven for every game: Baynham, Hawkes, McNally, Pacey, Owen, Groves, Bingham, Brown, Morton, Cummins and Gregory. It was not an easy route to Wembley and involved three replays. Leeds United were disposed of 5-1 at Kenilworth Road as were Leicester City 4-1 in a replay after 1-1 at Filbert Street. Next came Ipswich Town away which resulted in a 5-2 victory and the knackering of my Zundapp motorbike on the way back from Portman Road. Away to Blackpool there was a 1-1 draw and at the replay I was part of the all-time record crowd of 30,069 at Kenilworth Road who witnessed a 1-0 win (It was a bit tight at the Oak Road end). The semi-final was against Norwich City when I saw a 1-1 draw at White Hart Lane and in the replay I took it as a good omen when the coach (no motorbike remember) parked directly outside the house where my father had been born. I was right and Billy Bingham scored the single goal that would get us to Wembley on 2nd May.

One of the downsides of the cup run was probably the worst ever football song, sung by an Irish Lutonian to the tune of 'When Irish Eyes Are Smiling' which was inflicted on the home crowd before every match during the run.The first line was, 'When Luton get to Wembley, we'll all be there to see' but no we bloody wouldn't. The final was against Nottingham Forest who we had beaten 5-1 earlier so it would be easy wouldn't it? About as easy as getting a ticket, I tried everything, tried again and totally failed. So did Luton. Two nil down after fifteen minutes and despite breaking goal scorer Roy Dwight's leg (he was Elton John's uncle) in a Brendan McNally tackle all Town could manage was a Dave Pacey consolation goal late on. Allan Brown headed wide and Billy Bingham hit the side netting but it wasn't to be and poor old Bob Morton was with some cruelty dubbed, 'The only Cup Final centre-forward who never had a shot at goal'.Just before the final skipper Syd Owen had been unveiled as the next manager. He announced his retirement after the final and was voted Footballer of the Year by the press.

SEASON 1959-60

The disappointment of Wembley soon went away in a summer of glorious weather during which I played more cricket and drank more beer than in any summer before or since but worse was to come, bottom place and relegation to Division 2. Despite having virtually the same squad Luton lost half of their league games and won only nine. Gordon Turner lost his magic touch with only six goals in his 31 aooearances and Billy Bingham was top scorer with 16 goals from 40 games on the wing. Town scored four only once at home to Fulham but conceded four or more five times.

75

The team seemed totally aimless and I was moved to write a letter to the *Luton News* (probably my first published work) suggesting that Syd Owen should come out of retirement to 'Bring some inspiration to a spiritless team' (a bit naïve but I was young). He didn't and was sacked on 16th April 1960 as relegation became virtually certain. He later became a coach at Leeds United.The Hatters fared slightly better in the FA Cup with away wins against Exeter City 2-1 and Huddersfield Town 1-0 before being crushed 4-1 at Kenilworth Road by Wolverhampton Wanderers.In the Southern Professional Floodlit Cup there was a 1-1 home draw against Fulham who won the replay, which for some unknown reason was at Brentford rather than Craven Cottage, 1-0.

Seven players made Luton debuts during the season. None would have any impact on Town's future but a couple are worth a mention. Albert McCann played just six times but would go on to have a twelve year career at Portsmouth scoring 85 goals in 338 appearances and be installed in the club's 'Hall of Fame'. Michael Tracey had been an England amateur international and Luton was his only professional club. He played just 23 times before injury ended his playing career and he then trained to be a solicitor. In the middle of a succesful legal career he made the news in 1980 when he gave up everything to do a *'Good Life'* and attempt to live off the land on an Irish smallholding with his wife and twelve children!

SEASON 1960-61

In the close season former Charlton goalkeeper Sam Bartram was persuaded to leave the manager's chair at York City and come to Kenilworth Road.

Between 1934-56 he had made an incredible 579 appearances for Charlton Athletic and represented England in three wartime internationals. Luton would be his last management job and he became a succesful football columnist on *The People* Sunday newspaper. He just about stopped the slide and there was a 13th place finish back down in the second tier. There were some impressive wins at home the best being 6-1 versus Middlesborough with 4-1 scorelines against Southampton, Stoke City and Charlton and 4-2 against Bristol Rovers but Sunderland had sweet revenge for Luton's previous big wins with a 7-1 win at Roker Park. Gordon Turner was back on form with 29 goals and there were twelve other scorers but none made double figures.

In the FA Cup there was a 4-0 home win against Northampton Town but the game I remember most was the 4th Round tie at home to Manchester City. I watched as Dennis Law scored four at the Oak Road End and City were leading 6-2 when the referee decided to abandon the game due to the waterlogged state of the pitch. Law's goals were expunged from the records (couldn't happen to a nicer bloke) and Luton won the re-arranged game 3-1. Unfortunately Luton then lost to a single goal in the next round at Barnsley. A new competition was introduced, the Football League Cup, and Luton lost 5-2 to Liverpool in a replay after a 1-1 draw at Anfield.

This time eleven new players were used and many disappeared without trace but some were significant.

Full-back John Bramwell came from Everton as part of the deal that saw Billy Bingham leave Luton and would make 206 appearances. Harry Walden was signed from Kettering Town and would play 106 times playing on both wings and at inside forward before moving to Northampton Town in 1964. Stewart Imlach was signed for £8,000 from Nottingham Forest where he had scored 43 goals in 184 games, won four Scottish caps and also helped to beat Luton at Wembley. He had a street named after him in his native Lossiemouth but didn't make much impression at Luton playing just nine times. Goalkeeper Jim Standen was signed from Arsenal and in 1962 moved to West Ham where he won the 1963-4 FA Cup and 1964-5 European Cup Winners Cup. He was also a First Class cricketer with Worcestershire scoring over 2,000 runs and taking 313 wickets with his fast-medium bowling between 1959-70. He won a Championship medal in 1964 heading his county's bowling averages and also appeared as 12th man in England Test Matches.

SEASON 1961-62

A good first half to the season faded and mid-table 13th place was the result again. There were some good home scores including Preston 4-1, Derby County 4-2, Bury 4-0, Rotherham 4-3 and Swansea Town 5-1 but some bad ones too with losses 4-1 to Southampton and 6-1 to Charlton. Two good away results were 4-2 at Middlesborough and 4-0 at Norwich but there was a 4-1 reversal at St James Park Newcastle. Gordon Turner top scored again with 21 and Alec Ashworth, signed from Everton the previous season, contributed thirteen.

Ron Baynham and Jim Standen shared goalkeeping duties roughly equally throughout the season but in April with Jim Standen in goal, Ron Baynham turned out at centre-forward for a home game against Leyton Orient. The experiment was not a success and resulted in a 3-1 defeat.

In the FA Cup it took Ipswich Town three matches to get revenge for 1959. There were 1-1 draws away and then home meaning a second replay at a neutral venue. With some mates on a cold January evening I made my one and only visit to Highbury only to see Luton smashed 5-1. The League Cup was slightly more succesful with a 2-1 home win against Northampton and a 0-0 draw with Rotherham at Kenilworth Road before going out 2-0 at Millmoor. Two fowards of some note came in to Kenilworth Road, Fred Jardine was signed from Dundee and would make 243 appearances up to 1971 when he left for one season at Torquay United before ending his career at Ampthill Town. Tommy McKechnie played 146 times before leaving for Bournemouth in 1966. He had been on Rangers books but didn't get a game and was signed from the wonderfully named Kirkintlloch Rob Roy club. After the season end Sam Bartram left the club 'by mutual consent'.

SEASON 1962-63

Before the season start Luton appointed Jack Crompton as manager. He had played almost 200 times in goal for Manchester United, had come to Kenilworth Road as a trainer in 1956 but gone back to Old Trafford two years later following the Munich Air Disaster.

Just seven days after his appointment he resigned 'for health reasons' but went straight back to Manchester United where, apart from a brief spell managing Barrow, he stayed in various roles for many years. Crompton's replacement was Bill Harvey who had been at Grimsby Town but never got a first team game. After WW2 he had decided to concentrate on coaching and this was his first management job. Luton didn't score four in a game until November when they beat Walsall 4-3 and further home wins included Middlesborough 4-3, Norwich 4-2 and Charlton 4-1. At no stage did the Hatters concede more than three goals but there were just too many losses and the end result was last place and another relegation. Gordon Turner managed only 16 goals in 35 matches and top scorer was Ron Davies with 21 from 29 games.

Centre-forward Davies would be sold on after just three games of the next season and would go on to play 644 league matches for various clubs including Norwich and Southampton winning 29 Welsh caps. Winger Danny Clapton had played over 200 games for Arsenal but left Luton after just 11 games to play for Corinthians in Sydney, Australia. The only other debut of note was that of Gordon Riddick, a defensive midfielder who had come through the youth ranks and would go on to play 114 games and score 17 goals before moving to Gillingham in 1967 where he would also make over 100 appearances. There was a 2-0 home defeat against Swindon Town in the 3rd Round of the FA Cup but there was better progress in the League Cup. Drawn away in all three ties Luton beat Southport 3-1 and Barnsley 2-1 before going down 1-0 to Manchester City at Maine Road.

SEASON 1963-64

Only Ron Baynham, Bob Morton and Dave Pacey remained from the 1959 FA Cup Final team and both Morton and Gordon Turner were in their last season at the club. In the third tier for the first time since 1937 it was certainly a new era as it was for me personally as work took me away from Bedfordshire and live games would be a rare event in future. A division lower but only an 18th place finish. There were few highlights, a 4-2 home win against Southend saw Gordon Turner's last club hat-trick and a 6-2 win away at Brentford saw new hero John O'Rourke net four. He also had a hat-trick in the 4-2 win over Bristol Rovers. O'Rourke had been signed from Chelsea and it was his 22 goals in just 23 games that almost certainly saved Luton from successive relegations. His final tally for the club would be 66 goals from just 90 games and it was a sad day when he was sold to Middlesborough in 1966 for £18,500 where he continued his prolific scoring.

Bob Morton had played most of the season at full-back and right-half and he played the last of his record 562 appearances against Wrexham at Kenilworth Road on 11th April 1964. Bob had joined the Hatters in 1945, turning professional a year later and was aged 38 when he left, even then he didn't actually hang up his boots as he became player/manager at Bletchley Town for a spell. Gordon Turner scored his last goal for the club, a penalty, in the same game and his last match was on April 25th at home to Watford when he strangely played on the wing. In this 406th appearance he didn't add to his record 276 goals. He retired to run his sports outfitters shop in Luton with Wally Shanks but would die at the early age of 46 suffering from motor neurone disease.

Of the ten new players only two other than John O'Rourke would make serious contributions. Defensive midfielder John Reid was signed from Northampton Town and would appear 121 times before leaving for Torquay United in 1966. Ray Whittaker came from Arsenal without having made a first team appearance but for Luton he scored 45 goals in 188 appearances before moving to Colchester in 1969 and retiring from football at the very young age of 26. In the FA Cup it was back to having to enter at the 1st Round stage where there was a 3-0 win at Bridgwater Town followed by a 2-1 win at Kenilworth Road versus Reading before losing 4-1 to Fulham at Craven Cottage. In the League Cup Round 2 there was a narrow defeat 4-3 at home to Coventry City

SEASON 1964-65

The inevitable had only been delayed and relegation to Division 4 after finishing in 21st place was the end of season result, although Luton were top of the four teams going down! The season had started reasonably well with three wins in the first five games but a run of sixteen games without a win followed leading to the resignation of manager Bill Harvey. Charlie Watkins, a member of the coaching staff with over 200 Luton appearances under his belt took over in a caretaker role for about three months until the appointment of former manager George Martin. He had last been at the club from 1944-47 so it was hardly a forward looking move. Despite a run of four consecutive wins in March and April there would be no reprieve.

The only highlights had been home wins versus Brentford 4-2 and Barnsley 5-1 but there had been some horrendous away defeats at Gillingham 5-0, QPR 7-1, Exeter 5-1, Shrewsbury 7-2, Southend 5-0 and worst of all in the penultimate game of the season 8-1 at Scunthorpe. Top scorers were Tommy McKechnie with just 11 and John O'Rourke with 10 from 22 games. Luton reached Round 3 of the FA Cup with 1-0 home wins over both Southend and Gillingham but in another home tie went out 3-0 to Sunderland. In the League Cup there was a 1-0 away win at Port Vale but defeat by the same score at home to Aston Villa.

The last two members of the 1959 cup final team played their last games, Ron Baynham kept goal for the last time at London Road, Peterborough on 6th February, unfortunately without a clean sheet in the last of his 434 appearances since 1952. He earned three England caps but probably would have had more but for the strong competition from the likes of Ted Ditchburn, Reg Matthews and Alan Hodgkinson. Dave Pacey played his last game about a month later bringing his tally to 280 appearances and 19 goals including the one at Wembley. Two of the ten players making their debut would play a big part in the history of Luton Town. Winger David Pleat was signed from Nottingham Forest and would play 79 times and score 10 goals before departing to Shrewsbury Town but he would, in two future spells, be one of the best ever Luton managers and would also manage Leiceter City and Tottenham Hotspur. The other was midfielder Bruce Rioch who would score 52 goals in 167 appearances and play a vital part in Town's escape from the basement.

He left Luton, which was his first professional club, in 1969 and would make over 600 appearances for clubs including Aston Villa, Derby County and Everton, winning 24 Scottish caps and becoming the first English born captain of Scotland. On retirement he managed seven English clubs including Arsenal and two in Denmark.

SEASON 1965-66

Down in the basement of the Football League, Luton finished 6th but only missed promotion by one point, a win rather than a 1-1 draw at Chester in the last game of the season would have been enough. Four home wins all featured John O'Rourke hat-tricks, Barnsley 5-4, Crewe Alexandra 4-0, Chester 5-2 and Rochdale 4-1. A more unlikely goal provider was Tony Read who had been signed from Peterborough as a goalkeeper. Recovering from a broken foot, he had been given a run-out in the forward line in the Reserves to gain fitness and did so well that he was selected for the first team. He scored 12 goals including a hat-trick in the 5-1 defeat of Notts County before taking the goalkeeping jersey from Colin Tinsley and made 229 appearances before retiring in 1972. Other newcomers who would become firm favourites included John Moore a scottish defender signed from Motherwell who would make 306 appearances before moving on in 1973. He would come back to Kenilworth Road as a coach under David Pleat, would take over from Pleat for one season and then after a time away would come back to the coaching staff staying until his 60th birthday. Luton born midfielder Alan Slough who would play 312 times and score 32 goals became very popular with fans until his transfer to Fulham in 1973 and then Peterborough playing over 250 more league games.

Winger Graham French a former England Youth international from Shrewsbury was something special and something of a folk hero often said to start a match with a hangover from well documented drinking sessions which seemed to melt away as soon as he got the ball out on the wing where his pace, stamina and two-footed ability made him one of the best. He scored 23 goals in 202 appearances before his career was cut short by a three year prison sentence following a shooting incident (needless to say in a local pub). Luton gave him another chance on his release but he never made the first team again. After a brief spell at Reading and time in the USA, he finished his career at Southport under the assumed name of Graham Lafite. Another character making just six appearances before moving on was Bedford born Barry Fry who managed both Dunstable Town and Bedford Town before more famously taking charge at Birmingham City and Peterborough.

Both cup campaigns were best forgotten, in the League Cup a 1-1 draw at Kenilworth Road was followed by defeat 2-0 at Brighton and Hove Albion and in the FA Cup it took a replay to get past non-league Romford 1-0 and a replay after a 2-2 draw to get knocked out at home by non-league Corby Town. The drop to Division 3 and then to Division 4 meant that in a brief period Luton played no less than twelve clubs for the first ever time competitively leading to some interesting experiences (not always of the pleasant kind) for loyal fans including my brother travelling to away games at some strange places. This was the season that Substitutes were permitted for the first time, only one and only for injury. Tactical substitutions were not allowed until 1967-68 and multiple substitutes were years away. Luton's first ever substitute was Bruce Rioch who came on in the third game of the season at Aldershot.

Substitute appearances, however brief, now counted as appearances which puts the three, four and five hundred appearances of players in the pre-substitute days into context.

SEASON 1966-67

The promise of the previous season disappeared, as did John O'Rourke sold to Middlesborough before the season started and the result was a lowly 17th place out of 24. The only highlights were 4-0 home wins against Aldershot and Exeter City and 5-1 versus York City. York reversed the result winning 5-1 at Bootham Crescent but the absolute low was being thrashed 8-1 at Lincoln when the Imps were bottom of the table and despite Luton having a new manager. After a run of eight matches without a win George Martin had been sacked and was replaced by another former Luton player Allan Brown. Scottish International Brown had moved to Portsmouth on leaving Kenilworth Road and then in 1964 became player/manager of non-league Wigan Athletic until accepting Luton's offer on 4th November 1966.

Among new acquisitions was former England centre-forward Derek Kevan from Peterborough. Derek Tennyson Kevan had scored 157 goals in 262 league appearances for West Bromwich Albion winning fourteen England caps and also netted 48 in 67 for Manchester City. Very much in the twilight of his career, he only managed six goals in twelve games for Luton before being sold to Stockport County in a deal which brought Keith Allen to Kenilworth Road and he would score 43 in 154 appearances before leaving for Plymouth Argyle in 1970.

The only other newcomer of note was Max Dougan from Leicester City who would play 132 times in central defence before he too left in 1970 for Bedford Town. In the FA Cup there was a 2-0 replay win over Exeter after a 1-1 result at St James Park but then a 3-2 exit away to Bristol Rovers. The League Cup also involved a replay with a 2-2 draw at Aldershot being followed by a 2-1 defeat at Kenilworth Road.

SEASON 1967-68

Champions! and on the way back up. A string of eight consecutive wins in October/November set the tone and included 5-0 away at Exeter and home wins against Doncaster 5-3, Workington 4-0 and Swansea Town by the same score. Luton went to the top of the table on 17th February with a win at Brentford and stayed there for the rest of the campaign. The Championship was clinched with three games to spare with a 4-0 home win against second placed Crewe. Two signings made a significant contribution, central defender Terry Branston who had made almost 250 appearances for Northampton Town was immediately made captain by Allan Brown and would play 118 times for Luton before leaving for Lincoln City in 1970. Inside forward Ian Buxton who had made 145 league starts for 2nd Division Derby County was signed for £11,000 and chipped in with 14 goals. Buxton was also a First Class cricketer for Derbyshire scoring over 11,000 runs and taking 483 wickets in a career that spanned 1959-73. It was manager Brian Clough objecting to Buxton also playing cricket that made him available to sign for Luton and he played over 50 games before moving to Notts County in 1969. Bruce Rioch was top scorer with 27 goals and 16 were contributed by Keith Allen.

Others who were virtually ever-present in a fantastic season were Tony Read in goal, Scotsmen Max Dougan and Fred Jardine mostly at full-back, half-backs Alan Slough and John Moore and Ray Whittaker who contributed 10 goals from the left wing. Right wing duties were shared between Graham French and John O. Ryan (not to be confused with John G. Ryan who was yet to arrive on the scene). The FA Cup saw a home win against Oxford City before defeat 3-2 to Swindon at the County Ground and in the League Cup Charlton were beaten 2-1 in a replay at The Valley after a 1-1 result at home but this was followed by exit at Elland Road losing 3-1 to Leeds United.

SEASON 1968-69

Back to back promotions were missed by just three points despite beating champions Watford on the last day of the season in front of the best crowd since 1961 of 25,253, a 3ʳᵈ place behind Swindon Town was all that could be achieved. The season had opened with a 4-0 win against Oldham at Kenilworth Road and other home highlights included Barnsley 5-1, Mansfield 4-2, Barrow 5-1 and Stockport 4-1. Cash was available and signings included defender Jack Bannister from Crystal Palace who would play almost 100 time for Town before leaving for Cambridge United. Sandy Davie came from Dundee as back-up for goalkeeper Tony Read, he would later emigrate and be capped eleven times for New Zealand from 1979-81. Big money was spent on Brian Lewis from Coventry City and he rewarded the investment with 22 league goals. Welsh centre-forward Laurie Sheffield came from Oldham Athletic, he had more clubs than golfer Lee Westwood, Luton was his eighth and more were to follow.

Probably the most significant was Mike Keen who had made 393 league appearances for Queens Park Rangers and would make 160 for Luton before leaving for Watford in 1972 where he would make 126 more becoming player/manager and then manager.

In the week before Christmas, Allan Brown was sacked as manager for 'disloyalty', all he had done was to apply for the vacant job at Leicester City (which he didn't get). The following day he was replaced by Alec Stock the former QPR manager. Brown was very quickly snapped up by Portsmouth. Somerset born Stock had played just 30 league games for QPR before WW2 and was later player/manager at non-league Yeovil Town. There he was in charge for Yeovil's famous 1949 cup run when they beat Bury and Sunderland before losing to Manchester United in the 5th Round. Stock was in charge at QPR when they became the first Division 3 team to win the League Cup and also led them to successive promotions to Division1. He is said to have been the inspiration for the *Fast Show* TV character '*Ron Manager*'. In the League Cup Watford were beaten 3-0 at Kenilworth Road and Brighton 4-2 also at home after an away draw but there was defeat in the 3rd Round 5-1 to Everton at Goodison Park. The FA Cup saw home wins against Ware Town 6-1 and Gillingham 3-1 before a 1-0 exit at Maine Road against Manchester City.

SEASON 1969-70

Second place and promotion to Division 2 with highlights for home fans being wins against Bristol Rovers 4-0, Bradford City 5-0, Doncaster Rovers 4-0 and Reading 5-0. In July 1969 crowd favourite Bruce Rioch was sold to Aston Villa for a reported £100,000, a record at the time for a third division club.Less than a week later £17,500 of that cash had been spent on an unknown full-back from Fulham. By the end of the season, that full back would have played up front in every league and cup game, scored 28 goals and ensured Luton's promotion. His name was Malcolm MacDonald. SuperMac would score 58 goals from just 101 games before his inevitable sale. At Newcastle he scored 95 times in 187 league games and at Arsenal 42 in just 84 matches. He gained 14 England caps netting six times with five of those scored in one game against Cyprus. A knee injury finished his career at the early age of 29 and he managed at Fulham and Huddersfield Town before moving to media work. Not bad for a full-back!

The Rioch cash also enabled other signings including striker Viv Busby from Wycombe Wanderers who made 86 appearances before moving to Fulham in 1973 where he made over 100 more. After football with his footballer brother Martyn and Luton team-mate Mike Keen he established a sports outfitters in High Wycombe. Striker Matt Tees came from Charlton Athletic and scored 13 goals in the season, in 2017 he was featured in a TV documentary on dementia when it was suggested that his advanced condition of the disease could be linked to heading the ball during his playing career.

An excellent central defender Chris Nicholl was signed from Halifax and I never saw him have a bad game. He made 106 appearances before being sold in 1972 going on to make over 200 appearances for both Aston Villa and Southampton and winning 51 caps for Northern Ireland. Last but by no means least was John G Ryan signed from Fulham who became something of a legend making 314 appearances in defence before moving to Norwich City in 1976. Another legend became connected to the club when comedian Eric Morcambe joined the Board of Directors on 31st January. The FA Cup performance was anything but legendary when a home replay win against Bournemouth was followed by an embarrasing 2-1 defeat away to Hillingdon Borough. In the League Cup Peterborough were beaten 5-2 in a Kenilworth Road replay after 1-1 at London Road, Millwall were beaten by the only goal at The Den after 2-2 at home but defeat followed in the 3rd Round 3-0 at Sheffield United.

SEASON 1970-71

A healthy start in Division 2 and 6th place finish was achieved with the highlights being home wins against Oxford United 4-0 and Orient by the same score with a 5-1 win away at Sheffield Wednesday. Twelve wins in the first half of the season slipped to six wins in the second half as form dipped. Malcolm MacDonald top scored with 30 from all competitions and newcomer Don Givens scored 13 times. Before the start of the season Graham French had been arrested following a shooting incident and on 4th December was sentenced to three year imprisonment.

Don Givens had been signed from Manchester United and would score 22 times in 91 appearances before transfer to QPR in 1972 where he would make almost 250 league appearances. He was capped 56 times by Republic of Ireland with 9 of those caps won as a Luton player. Also signed from United was Jimmy Ryan (not to be confused with John Ryan). Jimmy would make 204 appearances and score 25 times from the wing before moving to Dallas Tornado in 1976, he came back to Kenilworth Road on the coaching staff and would manage Luton in 1990-91.

Other signings included midfielder Peter Anderson from Hendon who would make 208 appearances and score 40 goals before his 1975 departure to Royal Antwerp. Luton born goalkeeper Keith Barber was signed from Dunstable Town and appeared between the sticks 158 times before his 1977 move to Swansea City. Luton also spent £30,000 on David Court who held the distinction of having played in every position except goalkeeper for Arsenal. Chairman Tony Hunt resigned on 9th March 1971 following the collapse of his V&G Insurance Company and as a result in May Malcolm MacDonald was sold to Newcastle United for an absolute bargain £160,000 to help balance the books.

SEASON 1971-72

This was very much a season of consolidation, only three players brought in and only nineteen players used all season with a mid-table 13th place the result. For the first season since at least WW2, Luton failed to score more than three goals in a match but on the plus side only one team did it to them, Blackpool 4-1 at Kenilworth Road.

Defender Alan Garner was signed from Millwall and would make 112 appearances before he was controversially sold to Watford in 1975 and would make exactly 200 league appearances for the Hornets. Gordon Hindson came in from Carlisle and striker Vic Halom from Fulham. Halom scored 17 goals in 63 appearances for Luton, was sold to Sunderland in 1973 and had an FA Cup winners medal with them less than three months later. A player who had been some time at the club was now making his presence known, former Fulham youth full-back Don Shanks would make 110 appearances before moving to QPR where he would play in 180 league games.

Luton crashed out of both the FA and League Cups at the first hurdle, 2-1 away to West Ham and 2-0 away to Crystal Palace. They did no better in a new competition sponsored by Watneys, the makers of the infamous Red Barrel bitter. The Watney Cup was a pre-season competition that only lasted three years and was between two teams from each of the four divisions selected on the basis of most goals scored without being promoted or qualifying for a European competition. Luton were away to Colchester United and lost 1-0. Colchester went on to win the competition which was noteworthy as being the first to settle drawn games by means of a penalty shoot-out. Two days before the last match of the season manager Alec Stock resigned. Less than a week later Harry Haslam who had played only nine league games and whose only managerial experience was a record 552 games and winning the Kent Senior Cup with non-league Tonbridge, was plucked from obscurity and given the job. He would lead Luton back to Division 1.

SEASON 1972-73

Luton moved up one place to twelfth and managed a 4-1 win at home to Huddersfield to cheer the fans. The squad had been strengthened with four players who would between them play over 800 times for Luton. Forward John Aston had played 155 times for Manchester United and would make 201 appearances and score 36 goals before leaving for Mansfield Town. Defender John Faulkner was signed from Leeds and would play 239 times for Town before his departure to Memphis Rogues in 1978. Full-back Bobby Thomson came from Birmingham City with eight England caps to his name and made 135 appearances. Central defender Paul Price was with Welwyn Garden City and played 230 times for Luton before being sold to Tottenham in 1981 for £250,000. He won 25 Welsh caps (2 while with Luton) and with Spurs played in the FA Cup and League Cup finals of 1982. Other signings included Barry Butlin from Derby County, Rodney Fern from Leicester and goalkeeper Graham Horn from Arsenal. Derek Hales was signed from Dartford and would play only nine times but went on to be Charlton Athletic's all-time highest goal scorer in two spells at the club.

There was a good run in the FA Cup and Luton eached the quarter-finals for the fourth time. Crewe were beaten 2-0 at Kenilworth Road before good away wins at Newcastle United 2-0 and Bolton Wanderers 1-0 with the run coming to an end 2-0 away to Sunderland. It took three games to get knocked out of the League Cup with 1-1 draws home and away against Birmingham City before defeat by the only goal in the 2nd replay at the County Ground Northampton.

In a competition new to the Hatters, The Anglo-Italian Cup, Luton beat Bari 4-0 at Kenilworth Road, lost 2-1 at Verona, beat Fiorentina 1-0 at home and drew 2-2 in Rome with Lazio but somehow didn't get past the qualifying rounds. The competition ran intermittently between 1970 to 1986 under various names but had a reputation for violence among fans established early when the very first final was abandoned due to fighting on the terraces and was awarded to Swindon Town.

SEASON 1973-74

A change of shirts for Luton from white to orange came as a shock to the faithful but brought second place and promotion to Division 1 only fourteen years after they left it on a journey all the way down to Division 4 and back again. It's the quickest it's ever been done (if indeed it has been done by anyone else but the Hatters). The shirts were orange with white and navy blue trim and worn with navy shorts The first game of the season was a 4-0 thumping at Nottingham Forest but this was followed by the best result of the season a 6-1 home win against Carlisle.There was steady good form throughout the fixture list and promotion was achieved with a 1-1 draw with WBA at the Hawthorns in the penultimate game of the season. The 4-3 reverse at home to Sunderland in the last game didn't matter as the Hatters were already up with Carlisle and champions Middlesborough. The cause was helped mid-season by Jimmy Husband who was signed from Everton and would score a hat-trick helping him on his way to the 48 goals he would score in 162 appearances. Northern Ireland international Tommy Finney was signed from Crusaders and scored five goals in his first five games but became a fringe player and left at the end of the season.

Much more significant was the arrival of Alan West from Burnley. West played every game from his signing, would be ever-present next season back in Division 1, would become club captain making 317 appearances, scoring 17 goals and in later years would be Luton Town's Chaplain.

Major contributions in this promotion season were also made by Graham Horn in goal, Bobby Thomson ever-present at full-back, Peter Anderson, John Faulkner and Alan Garner at half-back, John Aston, Jimmy Ryan and top scorer Barry Butlin with 18 goals. There were reasonable runs in both cup competitions with Port Vale beaten 4-2 in a Kenilworth Road replay in the FA Cup after a 1-1 result away, followed by Bradford City 3-0 at home but a 4-0 thumping by Leicester City also at Kenilworth Road in the 5th Round. In the League Cup it took three matches to get past Grimsby Town 2-0 in the 2nd replay after 1-1 and 0-0 scorelines home and away. A replay was also needed to beat Bury 3-2 away after no goals at home but defeat came at the Den with Millwall winning 3-2 in the 4th Round.

SEASON 1974-75

Disaster! In 20th place just one point below Spurs and straight back down again along with Carlisle who did the same thing and Chelsea. It was certainly a season of two halves, first half just one win and seven draws and second half ten wins and four draws. New signings included Steve Buckley from Burton Albion who took over from Bobby Thomson at full back for the second part of the season and would make 135 appearances before leaving for Derby County where he would make over 300 more.

Adrian Alston, British born but an Australian World Cup player who won 37 caps stayed for just one season before leaving for Cardiff City. The Futcher twins Ron and Paul were signed from Chester. Centre-forward Ron would score 43 goals in 133 appearances and in the off-season was also knocking them in for Minnesota Kicks in the USA. Defender Paul made 142 appearances and won an England U21 cap before he was sold to Manchester City in 1979 for £350,000 when he became City's then most expensive player (how times change!), twin Ron went too.Luton's main problem had been the lack of goals which was illustrated by the fact that Ron Futcher, Adrian Alston and Jim Ryan were joint top scorers in the league with just seven each.

Luton fell at the first hurdle in the FA Cup losing 1-0 to Birmingham City at Kenilworth Road in the 3rd Round. The League Cup was not much better with a narrow 1-0 home win versus Bristol Rovers being followed by exit 2-0 away to Sheffield United. In the Texaco Cup Luton drew at home with Southampton and lost away to West Ham 2-1 with a 2-2 draw away to Orient at Brisbane Road in the qualifying stages but failed to progress. This was the last year of the Texaco Cup's five year existence. The competition was for the teams in the top two divisions in England, Scotland and Ireland 'Who had just missed out on major honours'. I don't remember it either! The fact that Town had won three and drawn one of their last four league games did give some hope for the next season but not much.Manufacturers were now allowed to put their names on shirts so we now knew that the new orange shirts were made by *Admiral.*

SEASON 1975-76

Back in Division 2 and the slide was stopped with a respectable 7th place. There were only two high scoring games, a 4-0 home win against York City and a 5-1 victory at The Valley against Charlton. Once more the season ended very well with two draws and then three wins in the last five games. Four players signed in previous seasons came to prominence, Paul Price became a fixture in central defence and Brian Chambers who had come from Sunderland via just one game for Arsenal became a regular in midfield until his departure for Millwall after 82 appearances. Andy King, Luton born, had come through the youth ranks and scored 9 goals before being sold to Everton at the end of the season. King would return to Kenilworth Road in 1985-86 for a handful of games before moving into management at Mansfield and Swindon Town. Bedford born Pasquale 'Lil' Fuccillo would score 27 goals in 180 appearances before leaving for Southend via Tulsa Rednecks in 1983 after a contract dispute. He too would return to Kenilworth Road in various roles including manager.

Coming on as a substitute in the penultimate game of the season and making his full debut in the last game against Blackpool at Kenilworth Road was absolute Luton legend Ricky Hill. Londoner Hill would be part of the club for many years as player, manager and other roles. He was second only to Bob Morton with 436 league appearances and 508 overall with 65 goals and 3 England caps, spending virtually all his playing career at Kenilworth Road except for a few games for Le Havre and Leicester City at the end.

Not for the first time and certainly not for the last, the club was in financial difficulties mid-season leading to the sale of Peter Anderson to Royal Antwerp for a ridiculously low £55,000 fee and the release of Andy King at the end of the season. In the FA Cup a 2-0 home win against Blackburn Rovers was followed by defeat 2-0 at Carrow Road versus Norwich City. The League Cup saw immediate exit to lowly Darlington at Feethams.

SEASON 1976-77

Luton moved up one place to 6th and enjoyed some good wins at home against Bristol Rovers 4-1, Chelsea 4-0, Carlisle 5-0, and Notts County 4-2 who were also beaten 4-0 away. From 21st January there was a run of twelve wins and a draw which ensured a top half finish. Scottish international John K 'Dixie' Deans was signed from Jock Stein's Celtic where he had made 126 appearances and been a prolific goalscorer including six in one game against Partick Thistle. Unfortunately at Luton he only managed six goals in fifteen games before he was let out on two loan spells and then released moving to Australia to join Adelaide City where once again he became a prolific scorer. Goalkeeper Milija Aleksic, who despite his name was born in Stafford was signed from Plymouth to replace Keith Barber. He played 92 games in his three years at the club where the fans inevitably gave him the nickname 'Elastic'. He was sold to Tottenham for £100,000 and won an FA Cup winners medal there but was replaced when Spurs signed Ray Clemence from Liverpool. Elastic came back to Kenilworth Road on loan playing four games in 1981 and not long afterwards emigrated to South Africa.

The Hatters benefitted from a settled team all season with Steve Buckley, John Faulkner, Paul Futcher and Paul Price all appearing in forty or more of the fortytwo league games. Price had been at centre-half in the previous season but made the right-back spot his own winning eleven of his 25 Welsh caps in this position while at Luton before being sold to Tottenham in 1981.Luton were drawn away twice in the FA Cup winning 1-0 at Halifax and then losing by the same score at Chester in the 4th Round. Also drawn away in the League Cup, Town went down 3-1 at Sunderland.

SEASON 1977-78

Down to a mid-table 13th with the best performances being an away win 4-1 at Cardiff and home wins against Sheffield United and Blackpool both 4-0 and the best in the third game of the season a 7-1 thrashing of Charlton with Jimmy Husband scoring four. Unfortunately he only managed three more in his seventeen other games and took no part in the latter half of the season. John Aston played just his 200th and 201st matches for Luton before being transferred to Mansfield Town. His replacement was Phil Boersma the former Liverpool man signed from Middlesborough who would contribute 11 goals in 40 appearances. He played just one game in 1978-79 before moving to Swansea City where his former Liverpool team-mate John Toshack was now manager

Another true Luton legend made his debut as a substitute in November, former youth player Brian Stein. Stein played most of the second half of the season and would go on to make 388 league appearances up to 1988 when he was a member of the League Cup winning team.

After a spell playing in France he returned in 1991-92 and took his final tally to 496 appearances in all competitions and 154 goals putting him in third place for Luton for both league appearances and goals scored. He would later undertake various roles at Kenilworth Road including caretaker manager. On 23 January Harry Haslam resigned to manage Sheffield United and the following day saw the appointment of former Luton player David Pleat who had finished his playing career at Peterborough in 1971 since when he had been managing Nuneaton Borough. At Sheffield United Haslam became the second English manager to sign a player from Argentina. He had gone to Argentina hoping to bring back a little known 17 year-old called Diego Maradona but had to settle for Alejandro 'Alex' Sabella from River Plate. Unfortunately Sabella didn't rise to the heights of Ossie Ardiles and Ricky Villa at Spurs. In the FA Cup a 1-1 draw with Oldham Athletic was followed by a replay win 2-1 at Boundary Park but Town were hammered 4-0 in the 4th Round against Millwall at The Den. The League Cup saw a good 3-1 win away to Wolves followed by three games against Manchester City. There were draws home and away before City won 3-2 at the 'neutral' venue of Old Trafford!

SEASON 1978-79

Pleat's new broom swept really clean, gone were John Aston, Steve Buckley, Paul & Ron Futcher, John Faulkner and Jimmy Husband and no less than seven players made their Luton debut in the first game of the season. There were some excellent buys among them.

Pleat's first signing was Mark Aizlewood for £50,000 from Newport County who would play 110 times in Luton's defence winning two Wales U21 caps before moving to Charlton in 1982 and winning 39 full Welsh caps at various clubs. David Moss cost £110,000 from Swindon Town which proved to be a bargain as he scored 94 goals in 245 appearances for Luton. Former Birmingham City favourite Bob Hatton was signed from Blackpool where he had scored 32 goals in 75 league games and did almost as well for the Hatters with 31 from 90 appearances. From his former club Nuneaton Pleat brought in Kirk Stephens (not to be confused with snooker player Kirk Stevens) Our Kirk would appear 248 times in Luton's defensive line-up. Probably the most significant signing was Mal Donaghy who would make 4th place in Luton's list of league appearances behind Bob Morton, Ricky Hill and Brian Stein with 415 (488 in all competitions).He was bought from Larne for just £20,000 and would become Luton's most capped player with 58 Northern Ireland caps while at the club and 91 altogether. After ten years he was sold to Alex Ferguson's Manchester United for £650,000 but played five more games for Luton in a loan spell in 1989-90.

Less succesful of the seven were Chris Turner from Peterborough via New England Tea Men who stayed only one season and 34 games before leaving for Cambridge who he later managed and former Manchester City youth player Steve Sherlock who played only two games before being sold to Stockport County where he was much more of a hit making 245 league turn-outs. Mid-season goalkeeper John W 'Jake' Findlay was signed from Aston Villa to take the place of Elastic Aleksic and would go on to play 187 times.

Another signing who made only ten appearances was the Leicester legend Alan 'The Birch' Birchenall. He later became Leicester's club ambassador and pre-match host and was made an Honorary Freeman of the City.

The seven debutants made a good start to the season with a 6-1 home win against Oldham and the good start continued with wins against Cardiff City 7-1 and Notts County 6-0 but form slumped later in the season and the result was a disappointing 18th place in the league. The FA Cup saw a 3rd Round exit 2-0 away to York City but there was better luck in the League Cup with home wins against Wigan Athletic 2-0 and Crewe 2-1 and a good away win 2-0 at Aston Villa before exit in the 5th Round 4-1 to Leeds at Elland Road.

SEASON 1979-80

Davis Pleat's team became very settled with eleven players involved in 39 or more of the 42 league games and a much improved 6th place resulted. The highlights were home wins against Swansea City 5-0 and Fulham 4-0 with the best away result being a 4-1 win at Charlton. One new signing who played in all but one league game was Londoner Tony Grealish from Leyton Orient. He played 86 games for Luton and won 17 of his 45 Republic of Ireland caps before leaving for Brighton & Hove Albion. One change however had been back to white shirts, albeit with orange trim worn with white shorts with orange trim and now made by *Adidas*. Before the season was over Luton had a sponsors name on those shirts for the first time , Dunstable based motor and coach company *Tricentrol* who are said to have paid £50,000 for the priviledge.

Other new players included Luton born midfielder Wayne Turner who would make 102 appearances and later become a coach and then assistant manager at Kenilworth Road. Defender Clive Goodyear signed from Lincoln City was one game short of being a centurion when he left for Plymouth Argyle where his did make it to 100 plus games. Later when with Wimbledon he played in the 1988 FA Cup final versus Liverpool and was the man who gave away the controversial penalty that keeper Dave Beasant famously saved. Two more not quite making the hundred were centre-half Mike Saxby from Mansfield Town and Steve White from Bristol Rovers. Centre-forward White would score 26 goals in 83 appearances and would be ever-present in the 1981-82 promotion season. There was early exit from the FA Cup beaten 2-0 at home by Swindon. The League Cup exit was almost as quick but for the first time was played over two legs and Town could not recover from a 3-0 defeat at Gillingham only managing a 1-1 draw in the return match.

SEASON 1980-81

There was a slight inprovement in league position up to 5th but the main problem seemed to be scoring goals with only two scores over three, 4-2 at home to Preston North End and the same score away to Bristol Rovers. Four players were tried at centre-forward, Frankie Bunn managed one in three starts and would only take his tally to 12 in 59 appearances before he left for Hull City in 1985. His later claim to fame was scoring six for Oldham in a 7-0 win against Scarborough, which still stands as a record individual tally for a League Cup match.

Andy Harrow signed from Raith Rovers failed to score in his four appearances and soon went back over the border to Alex Ferguson's Aberdeen. Former youth player Luton born Godfrey Ingram had a longer run but netted only five and the top scorer among those wearing the number nine shirt was Steve White with just seven. Chipping Sodbury born White went back to Bristol Rovers via Charlton before making over 200 appearances for Swindon Town and becoming a firm favourite at the County Ground. His son Joe also played for Rovers. Top scorer in the league by far was Brian Stein with 18.

One significant signing was Jugoslav internation Radomir 'Raddy' Antic who came from Real Zaragoza and ended his playing career with 108 appearances and 10 goals from midfield for the Hatters. A W H Smith that didn't make the news was Herbie Smith who came on as a substitute in a League Cup game and was never heard of again. The early rounds of the League Cup were again over two legs and Luton beat Reading 3-1 on aggregate before losing 2-1 at home to Manchester City in the single leg 3rd Round. There was two away ties in the FA Cup with Orient beaten 3-1 before defeat 2-1 to Newcastle United.

SEASON 1981-82

With a record of Won 25, Drawn 13 and Lost 4, Luton could only be Champions and back in Division 1 having topped the table for most of the season.

Among those many wins were 6-0 against Grimsby, 4-1 versus Shrewsbury and the most satisfying 4-1 against Watford.Mal Donachy, Kirk Stephens, Steve White and Brian Stein played every league game. Stein top scored with 21 goals and Steve White had 19 with David Moss on 16. Brian 'Nobby' Horton who had been signed from Brighton missed only one game and would go on to make 132 appearances for the Hatters. Horton had previously made 200 plus turn-outs for both Brighton and Port Vale and would go on to manage seven league clubs including Manchester City and is one of the few to have managed teams in the league for over one thousand games. Fellow midfielder Raddy Antic became something of a super-sub with thirteen of his thirty games being from off the bench. Antic would later become the only person to have managed all three of Real Madrid, Athletico Madrid and Barcelona and would also manage the Serbian national team.

Mark Aizlewood was sold to Charlton in March and Richard Money (aka Dickie Dosh) came in from Liverpool to take over at left-back. Money is another player who would return to Kenilworth Road as manager. There were two home ties in the FA Cup with a 2-1 win against Swindon Town being followed by a 3-0 defeat by Ipswich. The League Cup had a sponsor for the first time, the Milk Marketing Board and became known as the Milk Cup. Luton lost 2-1 to Wrexham in the two-legged tie.The second game of the season was the first ever league game played on an artificial surface. Luton beat QPR 2-1 and spoiled the Loftus Road party. Luton would soon get their own plastic pitch and spoil a lot more parties. Luton automatically set a points record in the league as this was the first season of 3 points for a win.

SEASON 1982-83

Something of a reality check for Luton back among the big boys with 18th place and survival depending on the last game of the season at Maine Road Manchester. Town won 1-0 keeping them up and sending City down and giving all those present or watching highlights on TV the never to be forgotten sight of David Pleat dancing onto the pitch at the end in a horrible brown suit. The season had started quite well with home wins against Notts County 5-3 and Brighton 5-0 and a 4-4 draw away at Stoke but the rot set in and there were some horrible losses to Everton 5-1 at home and 5-0 away, to Arsenal 4-1 and worst of all 5-2 to Watford. The big signing at the start of the season had been Paul Walsh from Charlton for £400,000 plus Steve White. He scored a hat-trick in his second game, played all but one league games, contributed thirteen goals and was voted PFA Young Player of the Year. Walsh won all five of his England caps in his two seasons at Luton and before his sale to Liverpool. He is now one of a number of ex-Luton players who are pundits on *Sky Sports*. Brian Stein made only 20 starts but still top scored with 14 goals.

Two players who had been at Kenilworth Road since the late 70s came through to play more regularly, central defender Clive Goodyear and Luton born attacking midfielder Wayne Turner. Paul Elliot was signed from Charlton, he was an England U21 international and later in life would be awarded the MBE and CBE for services to diversity and anti-racism in football. For the last twelve games of the season Pleat brought in loan players Tony Godden who had played over 250 times in goal for West Bromwich and Trevor Aylott from Millwall. They helped Town achieve the three wins and four draws that kept the team in Division 1

Almost under the radar in mid-season.a local lad played four debut games in defence, This was Mitchell Thomas the defender who in two spells separated by time at Spurs and West Ham would make 341 appearances for Luton. The Hatters were again drawn at home for their two FA Cup ties beating Peterborough 3-0 but losing 2-0 to Manchester United. There was a little bit of a run in the Milk (League) Cup with 3-2 aggregate win against Charlton and a 4-2 win at home to Blackpool before a narrow 1-0 loss to Spurs at White Hart Lane.The season saw the first change of shirt sponsor to *Bedford Trucks*, the commercial arm of Vauxhall Motors and Luton based since 1929. The white shirts now had orange sleeves.

SEASON 1983-84

There was a very slight improvement in league position up to 16th with a few good wins including home to Sunderland 4-1 and Wolves 4-0 and away to Stoke 4-2 but these were more than cancelled out by losses at home to Coventry 4-2 and Manchester United 5-0 and away to Spurs 4-2 and Liverpool 6-0 but the most telling statistic was just three wins in the last 23 matches. Paul Walsh was top scorer with only 14.There were debuts for a number of players two of which at least come into the legend category.Goalkeeper Les Sealey was signed from Coventry City, played every game of the season keeping twelve clean sheets and would make 259 appearances before moving on to other clubs including most notably Manchester United. He would die tragically young at just 47 from a heart attack. Former apprentice Tim Breacker made just two appearances but he would play another 260 times for Luton before signing for Billy Bonds at West Ham and making 240 appearances there.

Chukwuemeka 'Emeka' Nwajiobi came in from Dulwich Hamlet and became a great crowd favourite scoring 20 goals in 87 appearances and winning four caps for Nigeria before injury ended his playing career. Defender Rob Johnson had signed at a teenager some years before but a serious injury had slowed his development and only now did he start to notch up the 126 appearances he would go on to make. Mark Stein, brother of Brian make a solitary appearance but he would play over 100 games in two spells at Kenilworth Road twelve years apart. Both cups saw falls at the first fence, in the Milk (League) Cup the Hatters lost 4-3 on aggregate to Rotherham and in the FA Cup Watford were taken to a replay with a 2-2 scoreline at home but the replay at Vicarage Road was lost 4-3. In February England manager Bobby Robson picked both Paul Walsh and Brian Stein to play France in Paris. Unfortunately the duo failed to score and England lost two-nil.

SEASON 1984-85

There was a dreadful start to the season with only five wins from 25 games but eventually 13th place was achieved. A slight kit change saw Town playing in white shirts with blue trim, the sponsors name reduced to just *Bedford* and shorts were now blue.Two new signings started the season, goalkeeper Andy Dibble came from Cardiff City and would win three Welsh caps in his fairly brief time at Luton before keeping over 100 times for Manchester City. Dibble is probably best remembered for the 1988 League Cup final when he was standing in for injured Les Sealey and saved a crucial penalty when Luton were 2-1 down.

Former Manchester United midfielder Ashley Grimes came in from Coventry and won two of his 18 Republic of Ireland caps while chalking up 114 appearances for Town but neither featured in the first team after November and it was the four big money signings from December onwards who came straight into the team and saved the season. All four became real favourites and all four probably qualify as Luton legends.

England international central defender Steve Foster came fom Aston Villa and had previously been at Brighton where he won three caps and appeared in the FA Cup final. He would make 212 appearances for Luton and skipper them in the League Cup final. In 2008 he was named as part of the business consortium that took control at Kenilworth Road. Peter Nicholas was bought from Crystal Palace and made 116 Luton appearances winning 15 of his 73 caps in midfield for Wales while at the club. Wide player David Preece came in from Walsall and would end in the top ten of league appearances and play 395 times overall scoring 27 goals. Unfortunately he was another to die very young in 2007 aged just 44 some time after having surgery for throat cancer. Certainly a legend was Mick Harford, signed from Birmingham City for £250,000 who would score 92 goals in 217 games in two spells with Luton and win two England caps. He would subsequently serve the Hatters in many roles including coach, director of football, director of recruitment and was manager when Town played at Wembley in the Football League (Johnstone's Paint) Trophy in 2009.

As well as signing some very good players, David Pleat also took Luton to the semi-final of the FA Cup for only the second time in their history. Stoke were beaten 3-2 in an away replay after 1-1 at Kenilworth Road, also at home was a 2-0 win against Huddersfield and then it took three games to dispose of old rivals Watford 0-0 at home, 2-2 away and 1-0 in the 2nd replay. Millwall were beaten 1-0 at home to put Luton into the semi-final at Villa Park against Everton. Luton were 1-0 up with five minutes to go and could and probably should have had more. Everton equalised from a very dubious free kick and then scrambled a winner in the last few minutes of extra time. In the Milk (League) Cup Orient were beaten 7-2 on aggregate and Leicester 3-1 at home before exit 4-2 away to Sheffield Wenesday.

Some big names made very brief appearances for Luton, Micky Droy who had played 272 league games for Chelsea played 3 games on loan and Colin Todd who had played more than 300 games for Derby County and won 27 England caps came in from Vancouver Whitecaps to also play three games which were the last of his career. The quarter-final cup tie against Milwall was marred by an unprecedented level of crowd violence film of which was shown all over the world. In today's terms, it 'went viral' and would eventually lead to Luton imposing a ban on all away supporters in 1986.

SEASON 1985-86

On 17th August in the opening game of the season, Brian Stein scored the first ever goal on Luton's new plastic pitch in a 1-1 draw with Nottinhgam Forest. Queens Park Rangers had laid the first and two more would follow at Boundary Park, Oldham and Deepdale, Preston.

It was made of polypropyene tufts with a sand infill set in a porous shock pad and laid on an engineered base.Part of the plan was to make the ground a multi-event venue and there was some success when it hosted the first ever football international on an artificial surface, England v Northern Ireland (albeit at U15 level), several international hockey matches and a Barry McGuigan boxing match.It was during the plastic period that Luton flew highest winning the League Cup and achieving 7th in Division 1 their highest ever league finish. Some opponents were not so keen with Liverpool being the most vocal despite their two victories out of six on the surface. Defeats 4-1 and 3-1 were very much not appreciated by them and led to the question, 'What's the difference between a Boing 707 and Kenny Dalgleish ?' - answer, 'A 707 stops whining over Luton.' The plastic was dug up in 1991 and cut up into four inch square souvenirs, I still have mine,

The best performance of the season was on the plastic, a 7-0 win over Southampton with a Brian Stein hat-trick. There was a settled team with Mal Donachy playing every league game, Peter Nicholas and Mitchell Thomas missing only one and David Preece two. Mick Harford was top scorer with 25 in all competitions. There was only one signing of note, Mike Newell came from Wigan Athletic for £25,000 and would score 19 goals in 68 games before moving on to Leicester City. He would be back at Kenilworth Road as manager in the future. Two players from the youth ranks also made debuts and are worthy of a mention, Luton born Andy King scored 9 in 42 appearances but later made over 200 appearances for Everton. Marc North played just 24 games but went on to greater things at Grimsby and Leicester before succumbing to lung cancer at the tragically young age of thirtyfive.

The Milk (League) Cup saw a 5-2 aggregate win over Sheffield United before going out 2-0 at home to Norwich City. There was however another good run in the FA Cup starting with an away win 2-1 at Crystal Palace followed by a 4-0 home demolition of Bristol Rovers. It then took three games to get past Arsenal 2-2 home, 0-0 away and 3-0 in the 2nd replay back at Kenilworth Road. In the quarter-final there were two games against Everton 2-2 at home and exit 1-0 at Goodison Park.

SEASON 1986-87

Pre-season David Pleat left to become manager at Tottenham Hotspur and his job was given to former player and coach John Moore who would lead Luton to their highest ever league finish of 7th.It could have been better had Town not lost three and drawn one of their last five games. They could not have caught champions Everton who beat them in the last game of the season but the runner-up spot could have been a possibility. The ground had been further improved in the summer with the Kenilworth Road end terracing being covered, seating was installed in the Oak Road end and the Bobbers Stand was converted to executive boxes. It was however only the Luton faithful who saw these improvements as the controversial decision had been made to ban all away supporters from the ground in an attempt to stamp out the violence particulary prevalent in visits from Millwall and Watford. This did not go down well with the Football League and Luton were expelled from the League Cup which now had new sponsors and was known as the Littlewoods Cup.

The best results were home wins 4-2 against Nottingham Forest and 4-1 versus whingeing Liverpool with Mike Newell netting a hat-trick. There were few changes in the squad, defender Darron McDonough was signed from Oldham and made 127 appearances before he was sold to Newcastle United. He played just three games for the magpies before a snapped achilles tendon ended his career. Richard Harvey made his debut coming through the youth system and would have made many more than his 192 appearances but for a three year spell when he was dogged with injuries. Top goal scorers were Mike Newell with 13 Brian Stein on 12. In the FA Cup it took three games to dispose of Liverpool with a 3-0 win at Kenilworth Road after two games without a goal. In the 4th Round there was another draw at home 1-1 against Queens Park Rangers but defeat 2-1 in the replay on their plastic pitch.

SEASON 1987-88

Before the start of the season John Moore resigned after deciding that management was not the job for him. He had been a coach and would return in 1991 in a coaching role once more. His assistant and former Fulham manager Ray Harford (no relation to striker Mick) was given the role and would lead Luton into probably their best ever season. In the league there was a 9th place finish with highlights including wins 5-2 away and 7-4 at home against Oxford United and home wins against Portsmouth 4-1 and Newcastle United 4-0 although this was offset by a 4-2 defeat at St James Park. Five players, some of legendary status, made their debuts.

114

Luton born Kingsley Black came through the youth team and would play 156 times in midfield scoring 31 goals and winning 16 of his 30 Northern Ireland caps before Brian Clough took him away to Nottingham Forest for £1.5m. He would play over 100 games while at the City Ground and later even more at Grimsby. David Oldfield played just 39 league games before he was sold to Manchester City for £600,000 and then making well over 200 appearances for Leicester City before returning to Kenilworth Road to take his tally to 178 appearances and 32 goals. Danny Wilson was signed from Brighton and would win 15 of his 24 Northern Ireland caps while at Luton making 142 appearances and scoring 30 goals including a vital one in the League Cup final. He became a respected manager of eight clubs including both Sheffield teams and Barnsley twice.

Local boy Julian James was spotted playing for his home town team Tring Tornadoes and made his debut in central defence when he was just eighteen years old. He played a prominent part in the back line for over ten years clocking up 335 appearances before a reckless tackle by Barry Hayles of Bristol Rovers broke his leg in two places and virtually ended his career. Fellow defender Marvin Johnson was born within walking distance of Wembley Stadium but spent his whole playing career at Luton starting at youth level before making 439 appearances and 7th place in the all-time appearances list. He later managed the youth team of which he had been a member. This was to be the season when Luton got to Wembley twice and nearly three times.

The first was the Simod Full Members Cup which had been introduced in 1985 after English clubs had been banned from European competitions due to the behaviour of Liverpool fans at the Heysel Stadium disaster in Belgium where 39 people were killed. The Cup was open to teams in the top two divisions as opposed to the Associate Members Cup for 3rd and 4th division clubs.(Later known as the Football League Trophy and won by the Hatters in 2009). Luton got to the final beating Everton 2-1 away and with home wins against Stoke City 4-1 and Swindon 2-1 but almost 62,000 at Wembley watched Luton go down 4-1 against Reading.

There was also a great run in the FA Cup when Town were again semi-finalists beating Hartlepool 2-1 away, Southampton 2-1 at home, QPR in a home replay 1-0 after a 1-1 score at Loftus Road and finally Portsmouth 3-1 at home. In the semi-final at White Hart Lane Luton were unlucky to go down 2-1 to the Wimbledon 'Crazy Gang' who went on to famously beat Liverpool at Wembley and win the cup. Success finally came in the Littlewoods (League) Cup in which Town were again permitted despite away supporters still being banned from Kenilworth Road. Wigan were beaten 5-2 on aggregate and then the 'home' tie against Coventry was played at Filbert Street, Leicester so that away fans could attend to see Luton win 3-1. Ipswich were beaten 1-0 at Portman Road and Bradford City 2-0 at Kenilworth Road. The semi-final was back to two legs with Oxford United beaten 3-1 on aggregate.

Luton's opponents in front of 95,732 at Wembley were the hot favourites Arsenal. It was the Hatters whoever that opened the scoring with a Brian Stein goal and it stayed that way until substitute Martin Hayes and Alan 'Smudger' Smith scored in the 71st and 74th minutes to put the Gunners ahead. With just nine minutes left it looked all over when Arsenal were awarded a penalty but Andy Dibble making a rare appearance in place of injured Les Sealey saved it. A few minutes later Danny Wilson equalized and in the 90th minute Brian Stein smashed in the winner from a cross by substitute Ashley Grimes. The team that won Luton's first major trophy was Andy Dibble, Tim Breacker, Rob Johnson, Ricky Hill, Steve Foster, Mal Donaghy, Danny Wilson. Brian Stein, Mick Harford, David Preece, Kingsley Black (Substitutes Mark Stein and Ashley Grimes). I couldn't be there but as I watched on TV there were tears in my eyes as Steve Foster in his trade mark headband lifted the trophy.

SEASON 1988-89

It was very much a new look team with Dibble, Newell, Nwajiobi and the Stein brothers all gone. Goals seemed hard to come by with no-one making double figures in league goals and Danny Wilson and newcomer Roy Wegerle being joint top scorers in all competitions with just 12 each. Town slipped to 16th place in the league but there were some good performances at home with wins against West Ham 4-1, Southampton 6-1 and Charlton 5-2 but on the other side of the coin were away defeats to Wimbledon 4-0 and Liverpool 5-0.

Eight players made a debut and these included goalkeeper Alec Chamberlain signed from Everton who would play 159 times before leaving for Sunderland and later making over 250 appearances for Watford and becoming their goalkeeping coach. John Dreyer was signed from Oxford United and would become a firm favourite making exactly 250 appearances before being released in 1994 and joining Stoke City. Iain Dowie had an engineering degree and was combining working for British Aerospace and playing for non-league Hendon when he was signed. He would score 19 goals in just 78 games and win 5 of his 59 Northern Ireland caps before being sold to West Ham for £480,000. Later he would go into management and then become one of a number of ex-Luton players employed as pundits by *Sky Sports*.

South African born Roy Wegerle was signed from Chelsea and scored 18 goals in 59 appearances before QPR paid £1m for him. In 1991 he became an American citizen and subsequently wom 41 caps for USA. Defender Dave Beaumont came in from Dundee and featured in 91 games before returning north of the border to play for Hibernian and later a career as a police officer.England international Steve Williams was signed from Arsenal and had previously played over 300 times for Southampton in defensive midfield. The Simod (Full Members) Cup and the FA Cup both saw Luton eliminated at the first attempt in away ties at Crystal Palace 4-1 and Millwall 3-2 respectively.In the Littlewood (League) Cup however it was Wembley again! To reach the final Luton beat Burnley 2-1 on aggregate then Leeds United 2-0 at Elland Road followed by a home win 3-1 versus Manchester City.

It then took a replay to get past Southampton with a 2-1 away win after a 1-1 draw at Kenilworth Road.In the two leg semi-final West Ham were beaten 3-0 away and 2-0 home for a 5-0 aggregate score. In the Wembley final watched by 76,130 it was 1959 all over again but worse. Mick Harford headed a goal to give the Hatters a half-time lead but in the second half two goals including a penalty from Nigel Clough and one from Neil Webb gave the cup to Nottingham Forest!

SEASON 1989-90

Despite a record big money signing, Luton slipped to 17th place and were only saved from relegation by a 3-2 win at Derby County in the last game of the season. Manager Ray Harford was sacked in January and former Luton player Jim Ryan took his place. After his 200 plus games for Town, Ryan had moved to the USA playing for Dallas Tornado and Wichita Wings returning in 1984 to become manager of the Hatters Reserve Team. After leaving Kenilworth Road he held several management posts at Manchester United which had been his first professional club.Before the start of the season, Kenilworth Road had been sold to Luton Borough Council for a reported £3.25m and some of this was spent on the record signing of Danish International Lars Elstrup from Odense for £650,000 or even £850,000 according to some reports. This record buy was followed by a club record sale when QPR spent £1m on Roy Wegerle. Elstrup scored 27 goals in just 70 appearances in his two seasons at the club before being sold back to Odense for a bargain basement £200,000.(Even at the lower price of £650k, that's almost £17,000 per goal!)

The only other signing of note was Republic of Ireland international midfielder Mick Kennedy from Leicester City who stayed just one season before moving on to Stoke City. Three all from Wales and all who had come through the youth system made debut appearances. Forward Jason Rees would make 96 appearances and win one Welsh cap before departing for Portsmouth in 1994. Striker Kurt Nogan played 39 times and won two U21 caps for Wales and would go on to play over 100 times for both Brighton and Burnley. The third was Ceri Hughes who made 205 appearances, scored 20 goals and won 6 of his 8 Welsh caps while at Kenilworth Road.

The backbone of the team throughout the season however were Kingsley Black, Danny Wilson and David Preece who all missed very few games and Tim Breacker, John Dreyer and Alec Chamberlain who were all ever-present.Lack of goals was the problem illustrated by the fact that Kingsley Black top scored in the league with just 11 and that Town scored more than three only once in the league 4-1 at home to Norwich . In the FA Cup there was defeat 4-1 at Brighton and in the now even more catchily named Zenith Data Systems (Full Members) Cup there was a win 3-2 at Oxford and then a loss by 4-1 at Crystal Palace. Goals didn't seem to be a problem in the Littlewoods (League) Cup when Luton managed an 11-5 aggregate win over Mansfield Town but went out 3-0 at Everton. Five of those goals against Mansfield were from Lars Elstrup making his league goals even more expensive

SEASON 1990-91

A change of shirt sponsor to *Vauxhall* and maker to *Umbro* didn't help and Luton ended up even lower down the league in 18th place It was yet again a last game win against Derby County that saved Luton from relegation, this time 2-0 at Kenilworth Road. Scoring goals was once more a problem and only on three occasions did the Hatters score as many as three, 3-1 in a home win against Liverpool, 3-3 in a draw with Chelsea at Stamford Bridge and in a 4-3 defeat at Southampton. Lars Elstrup top scored with 15 in the league with the next best being seven each from Iain Dowie and Kingsley Black. There were new sponsors but no progress for Luton in the Rumbelows (League) Cup but they did for the first time in their history take part in a penalty shoot-out losing 5-4 on penalties to Bradford City after 1-1 scores home and after extra time away. In the Zenith Data Systems (Full Members) Cup there was a 5-1 win against West Ham at Kenilworth Road and a second penalty shoot-out, this time winning 4-1 on penalties after a 1-1 draw away at Chelsea but the run ended with defeat 3-1 to Crystal Palace at Selhurst Park. In the FA Cup there was a 3-1 win at Sheffield United and a 1-1 draw at home to West Ham before a 5-0 thrashing on the replay.

There were no signings of note but three came through from the youth training system who would make big names for themselves at Luton, elsewhere or both. Defender Matt Jackson played only 12 times for Town but he went on to play 138 times in the league for Everton and win an FA Cup winners medal, 161 league appearances for Norwich City and 167 for Wigan Athletic winning two promotions with them and later becoming their Head of Football Operations.

Defensive midfielder Mark Pembridge played 70 times and won three of his 54 Welsh caps at Luton going on to play over 100 games for all of Derby County, Sheffield Wednesday and Everton and also spending a season at Benfica. Right sided defender Paul Telfer made 165 Luton appearances and scored 22 goals before making more than 350 league appearances for Coventry City, Southampton and Celtic and winning a Scottish cap. Within days of the end of the season manager Jim Ryan was sacked.

SEASON 1991-92

With the departure of Jim Ryan, David Pleat was persuaded to return to manage the team but this time there was to be no last match reprieve, no brown-suited pitch dancing, this time it was 20th place, relegation and no participation in the new Premier League which was to be formed next season. Other decisions made before the start of the season were to rip up the plastic pitch and return to grass and to permit access to Kenilworth Road for away supporters once more. With the season just four games old and without a win the decision was also made to sell Kingsley Black to Nottingham Forest for a new club record £1.5m. There were no league highlights and Luton failed to score more than twice in any competitive game. There were however plenty of lowlights for long suffering travelling supporters including defeats at Coventry 5-0, Chelsea 4-1, Manchester United 5-0, Aston Villa 4-0, Tottenham 4-1, Manchester City 4-0 and Oldham 5-1. Brian Stein came back from France but scored just three goals in 39 games before leaving again.

All cup exits were swift, if not painless, defeat 4-0 in the FA Cup at Sheffield United, in the Rumbelows (League) Cup 5-4 on aggregate to Birmingham City and in the Zenith Data Systems (Full members) Cup lost on penalties after a 1-1 draw at Portman Road Ipswich. All this gloom was accompanied by the wearing of the most garish kit ever. Now sponsored by Bedfordshire based *Universal Salvage Auctions* the shirts were bright royal blue with white backs and fronts and emblazoned with a shield and zig-zag shapes in blue white and orange. They are now a collectors item worth up to £100 in new condition.

There was plenty of activity off the pitch, Trevor Peake came from Coventry City and would make 202 appearances in defence for Luton before becoming part of the coaching staff, Chris Kamara was signed from Leeds, spent two seasons at Kenilworth Road and would become yet another ex-Luton *Sky Sports* pundit (Unbelievable!). £180,000 was paid for Steve Thompson who had played over 350 games for Bolton Wanderers but after just seven appearances he was sold to Leicester City as part of the deal that brought Scott Oakes and Des Linton to Kenilworth Road. Scott Oakes was the son of Trevor Oakes of *Showaddywaddy* fame and would become a firm favourite making exactly 200 appearances and scoring 34 goals before transferring to Sheffield Wedenesday in 1996. Unfortunately his career was plagued by injury and he never achieved his obvious potential. His friend Des Linton would make 104 Luton appearances. Phil Gray was signed from Tottenham for £275,000 and scored 22 goals in just 59 league games before being sold to Sunderland for £800,000.

After playing over 100 times for the black cats he played in the Netherlands from where Luton bought him back in 1997 for £400,000 to bring his final tally to 53 goals in 161 games. In another showbusiness connection, Phil was the subject of the John Hegley poem *'A Gray Day'*. Two veteran goalkeepers came in on loan to fill-in for Alec Chamberlain in mid-season, Steve Sutton from Nottingham Forest and Mervyn Day from Leeds. Another loanee playing just 6 games was Imre Varadi making Luton the tenth of his 16 clubs (more clubs than any golfer you care to mention).

SEASON 1992-93

Luton had been relegated from Division 1 but were still in Division 1. the 'new' Division 1 that was the second tier below the Premier League.Town were not exactly exciting to watch in the league this season being involved in ten 0-0 draws and fourteen other games where they scored just a single goal. This puts the top scoring Phil Gray's 20 goals into context. Once again it all came down to the last games of the season, this time Luton lost to Sunderland but results elsewhere meant that they escaped another relegation ending in a lowly 19th place out of 24. Not only was the football a bit dull, the home kit had definitely been toned down by new makers *DMF* with plainer white shirts and navy shorts but still the same sponsor. Steve Claridge was signed from Cambridge but scored only 2 league goals in sixteen games before going back from where he came (in fairness he did score 4 goals in cup games).

His move to Luton was 7th in the 30 career moves Claridge made as a player (according to *Wikipedia*) putting Imre Varadi to shame (by having more clubs than any two golfers).

Luton also signed the one who got away. Kerry Dixon was Luton born and playing locally for Dunstable Town when he was signed by Reading for £20,000. After more than 100 games there he was signed by Chelsea for £150,000 plus another £25,000 if he ever played for England – he did eight times and became Chelsea's third highest ever goal scorer in all competitions with 193 after Bobby Tambling and Frank Lampard and clocking up 335 league appearances. For Luton although now approacjing his veteran stage, he would still score 20 goals in 88 games. The Hatters brought Australian U20 goalkeeper Andy Petterson to the UK. He played the first 14 games in place of Alec Chamberlain but made little impact and soon moved on. Julian James was now firmly established in defence alongside Darren Salton who had been a first choice defender since the start of the season. Salton had come to Luton as a youth trainee with friend and fellow Scot Paul Telfer and in November they were involved in a car crash in which a woman was killed. Telfer, who was driving, had minor injuries and missed only two games. Salton's leg injuries were such that he would never play again. The FA Cup saw a home win against Bristol City 2-0 followed by a 5-1 thrashing also at Kenilworth Road at the hands of Derby County. The League Cup had new sponsors yet again and in what was now the Coca Cola Cup Luton lost 5-4 on aggregate to Plymouth Argyle.

The Full members Cup was a thing of the past and there was a re-appearance of the Anglo-Italian Cup which had been going off and on since the 1970s. Luton managed draws against Watford away and Bristol City at home and were eliminated without ever seeing an Italian.

SEASON 1993-94

The Hatters were a bit more entertaining in the first part of the season with home wins against Burnley 5-0, Portsmouth 4-1 and Stoke 6-2 including a Kerry Dixon hat-trick. It didn't last and six defeats, three draws and only one win in the last ten games of the season meant a one place drop to 20th. As ever, when struggling, it was a problem to score goals and in the league no less than sixteen players scored but none made double figures (Kerry Dixon got a cup goal taking his total to 10). There were some notable first appearances, two coming through from youth football were goalkeeper Kelvin Davis and midfielder John Hartson. Davis, born in Bedford would play 107 times for Luton before moving on other clubs including Wimbledon and Southampton making more than 400 appearances for the two combined. John Hartson from Swansea having been sent home and then re-instated as a trainee for 'borrowing' his landlord's credit card, made 63 appearances and scored 13 goals before moving on to better things with Arsenal and West Ham United and winning 51 caps for Wales.

Juergen Sommer was brought from the USA where he had been Collegiate Goalkeeper of The Year at Indiana University. He started all but one game this season and would play 101 times and win three of his ten USA caps before moving to QPR becoming the first American goalkeeper to play in the Premier League.

He would no doubt have had more that his ten caps if he had not been around at the same time as Brad Friedel and Kasey Keller. Utility player Paul McLaren also came through the trainee system to make his first of 201 appearances before leaving for Sheffield Wednesday in 2001. Defender Mitchell Thomas made a welcome return to Kenilworth Road having played 157 and 38 league games for Spurs and West Ham respectively. In this second spell for Luton he would appear in 186 league games and bring his total in all competitions to 341. A certain Paul Dickov came for a loan spell from Arsenal and would later become more famous for his times at Leicester City and Manchester City. Midfielder Geoff Aunger was imported from Canada but played literally a handful of games. He moved on to Chester and Stockport but played even fewer there before returning to North America to play in both his native Canada and the USA. He finished his career with 44 caps for Canada. Five of those caps were won while he was at Kenilworth Road playing just five games for Luton. Five games, five caps, can't be bad!

In the Coca Cola (League) Cup there was defeat 2-0 on aggregate to Cambridge United and the Anglo-Italian Cup again produced no Italians when a 2-1 defeat at Watford and a 1-1 home draw with Southend United saw the Hatters eliminated in the preliminary rounds but in the FA Cup, despite the lack of goals and lack of league form, Luton reached the semi-finals.Southend United were beaten 1-0 at Kenilworth Road and Newcastle United were beaten 2-0 in a replay there after a 1-1 finish at St James Park. Cardiff City were beaten 2-1 away and it took another replay to put out West Ham 3-2 at home after 0-0 at the Boleyn Ground.

The semi-final was against Chelsea and I was 'up North' at a conference (work not political) and I remember wandering from pub to pub trying to find one with the game (live from Wembley) on TV, no chance with two Southern clubs involved. Apparently I didn't miss much as it was a prettty poor game with Chelsea winning 2-0. There was not much consolation when Chelsea lost the final 4-0 because it was Manchester United that did it.

SEASON 1994-95

Before the season started there had been a slight improvement at the ground with all of the Kenilworth Road end terracing being converted to seats. New shirts were unveiled which were white with an orange pinstripe and blue sleeves worn now with white shorts and obviously home made as the maker was *Hatter* (It didn't catch on, *Pony* got the job next season). The slight ground improvement was mirrored in league position at the end of the season which crept up to 16th despite the sale of John Hartson to Arsenal for £2.5million making him at the time Britains most expensive teenager . Highlights had been a satisfying win over Watford 4-2 at home where Middlesborough were also beaten 5-1 but there were some not so good performances losing 6-3 at home to Sheffield Wednesday and away at Grimsby 5-0 and Tranmere Rovers 4-2. Ten players had made their Luton debuts but only two of these would make any impression. Among the ten was Paul Allen who had played 444 league games for West Ham and Spurs and now played 4 on loan at Luton. When he was 17 he became the youngest player to be fielded in an FA Cup final now he was 32.

Another of very similar age was Gary Waddock signed from Bristol Rovers who had played over 200 league games for QPR and won 21 Republic of Ireland caps but far from past his best, he went on to make 178 appearances for Luton in defensive midfield before retiring in 1998 and going into management.

Striker Dwight Marshall was the other succesful signing coming from Plymouth Argyle he would score 38 goals in 155 appearances and was top scorer this season with 13 in all competitions but broke a leg the following season, never really reached his full potential after that and went back to Plymouth in 1998. Town fell at the first hurdle in the Coca Cola (League) Cup losing 4-3 on penalties after 1-1 scores home and away versus Fulham. In the FA Cup there were replays in both rounds played with a 1-1 draw against Bristol Rovers being followed by a 1-0 win away but in the next round after a 1-1 draw at Kenilworth Road there was a 6-0 thrashing by Southampton at St Marys.

SEASON 1995-96

Before the start of the season David Pleat left again this time to manage Sheffield Wednesday and his job was given to Terry Westley, a member of the coaching staff with no previous managerial experience and no playing experience at league level. Under him the team struggled to just four wins in 22 games and with a 4-0 defeat at Portsmouth being the last straw, he was sacked in the week before Christmas. Within days the job had been given to Lennie 'The Lion' Lawrence, another with no playing experience but with more than ten years experience as a manager at Charlton, Middlesborough and Bradford City.

He went on to be one of the exclusive few who managed more than 1,000 league games.There was a new manager 'bounce' of five wins and three draws but dire form returned, Luton ended up bottom and relegated to Division 2 (third tier). Incredibly during this dire season Luton used 35 players, enough for more than three teams, but although results were so poor some players did come into the team who would play a prominent part in the future of the club. Right back Graham Alexander was signed from Scunthorpe for just £100,000 and made 183 appearances and scored 17 goals before departing for Preston North End. He would go on to make exactly 400 appearances in two spells at Deepdale, 150 plus for Burnley and win 40 Scottish caps before moving succesfully into management. Steve Davis came from Burnley and would play 173 times and score 27 goals before returning to the Lancashire club and taking his appearances for them well over 300.

Attacking midfielder Stuart Douglas came through the youth team to score 23 goals in 172 appearances later training as a physiotherapist and doing that job at AFC Wimbledon. Striker Tony Thorpe a former Leicester City youth player had been on the fringes at Luton for a couple of seasons but came to prominence this season and went on to score 84 goals in 192 games in his two spells at Kenilworth Road. Bulgarian international Bontcho Guentchev was signed from Ipswich Town as a striker disappointedly finished with only 12 goals from 78 appearances but winning five of his 12 Bulgarian caps while at Luton before returning home to CSK Sofia. Another European player was Vidar Riseth who played just 12 games on loan before signing for Linz in Austria and winning 52 caps for Norway.

Luton also signed their second American international goalkeeper Ian Feuer, albeit with just one cap, but he played 115 times including a run of 90 consecutive games which was only ended by a shoulder injury. Darren Patterson was signed from Crystal Palace and made only 69 appearances but would win four of his 17 caps for Northern Ireland before being sold to Dundee. David Oldfield came back from Leicester for his second term at Kenilworth Road and would take his final tally to 32 goals in 178 appearances.

In the FA Cup Luton were humiliated 7-1 by Grimsby Town at Blundell Park and in the Coca Cola (League) Cup there was defeat 3-2 on aggregate to Bournemouth after extra time in the away leg. The Anglo-Italian Cup was notable for two things, firstly Luton actually got to meet some Italian clubs losing 4-1 at home to Perugia, 4-0 away to Genoa and 2-1 away to Cesena but beating Ancon 5-0 at Kenilworth Road. The second was the debut for Luton of former youth trainee Matthew Upson in the game at Cesena. In the following season Upson came on as an 88th minute substitute at home against Rotherham to make his one and only league appearance for the Hatters before being sold to Arsenal for £2million – not bad for a teenager who had only played 2 minutes plus added time. He would go on to a long and varied career with clubs including Birmingham City and West Ham and win 21 England caps. At the World Cup Finals in South Africa in 2010 he played as a central defender but joined Jermaine Defoe and Steven Gerrard as a scorer of one of England's pitiful haul of three goals.

SEASON 1996-97

A much better performance despite losing the first three games including a 5-0 to Bristol City at Ashton Gate. There followed a season with 21 wins the best being at home to Crewe 6-0 with a Tony Thorpe hat-trick and Preston 5-1 with a David Oldfield hat-trick. Thorpe was top scorer by a long way with 31 goals in all competitions. The end result was third place and a place for the first time in one of those bitter-sweet competitions, a promotion play-off. These had been introduced in 1987 but in all the time since then Luton's interest had been at the other end of the table. There was much less of a merry-go-round of players and only one debut of note among the four new players used. Panos Andrew 'Andy' Fotiadis came through the youth training system and would make 146 appearances and score 19 goals in his time at Kenilworth Road. He was dogged by injuries and never reached the potential that his early game promised and he eventually ended his career at Peterborough

In a lower Division the Hatters were now having to start the FA Cup in the first Round rather than Round 3 but they did at least reach it with wins at Torquay 1-0 and home to Boreham Wood 2-1. A 1-1 draw against Bolton Wanderers at Kenilworth Road was followed by a bit of a lesson and a 6-1 defeat in the replay in one of the last games played at Burnden Park before Bolton's move to a new stadium. Entry into the Coca Cola (League) Cup was also a round earler and Luton beat Bristol Rover 4-2 on aggregate and Derby County 3-2 also over two legs before a draw with Wimbledon in the 3rd Round. The replay was lost 2-1 at Kenilworth Road after extra time.

Being in the third tier also meant participation in the Auto Windscreens Shield (Associate Members Cup) where a 2-1 home win against Leyton Orient was followed by a 1-0 exit away to Northampton Town. The promotion play-off was in mid- May and finishing third meant Luton would play sixth place Crewe Alexandra, not a problem surely, hadn't we put six past them at home and kept a clean sheet away. But problem it was with a 2-1 defeat away and a 2-2 draw at Kenilworth Road meaning third tier football again next season. Crewe went on to beat Brentford in the final and clinch promotion from that sixth place five points short of Luton.

SEASON 1997-98

Luton slumped back down to 17th place and there were some big losses away to Wrexham 5-2 and Fulham 4-1 and at home to Bristol Rovers 4-2 and worst of all Watford 4-0. It was only a late run of six wins and seven draws in the last seventeen games that prevented a much nastier situation. Tony Thorpe was top scorer with 17 and among the fifteen other goalscorers only David Oldfield made double figures with eleven. Around a dozen players made their debut some of which are well worth a mention. Gary Doherty came through the youth ranks and scored 15 goals in 83 appearances before being sold to Tottenham in 2000 afterwards playing over 200 games for Norwich City and winning 34 Ireland caps. Another youth product was Luton born Ireland U21 international Liam George who scored 25 goals in 124 games before moving to Clydebank in 2002. Yet another former youth player would become a legend, Matthew Spring would make exactly 250 league appearances before being sold to Leeds United in 2004.

Matt returned to Kenilworth Road via Watford in 2007 and would make tenth spot in the top league appearances list with 308 and a tally of 43 goals in 357 appearances overall before leaving for Charlton Athletic in 2009.

Kelvin Davis and Ian Feuer shared goalkeeping duties but Andy Dibble was signed from Cardiff City and played just one league game this season. He would only play 39 times for Luton but won two of his three Welsh caps before moving to play over 100 games for Manchester City. Centre-back Alan White was signed from Middlesborough and sold to Colchester in 2000 where he would play over 150 games but returned to Kenilworth Road in 2009 to take his Luton tally to 114 appearances. A young striker Rory Allen played just 8 games on loan from Tottenham, the following year Spurs sold him to Portsmouth for £1million. Eight operations on knees and ankles later he retired at the age of 25 having played just 15 games for Pompey scoring only three very expensive goals. In the FA Cup there was defeat 1-0 at home to Torquay United and in the Coca Cola (League) Cup after a win on aggregate 2-1 versus Colchester Town went down 5-3 on aggregate to West Bromwich Albion. There was a mini run in the Auto Windscreens Shield (Associate Members Cup) when there were wins 2-1 at home to Brentford and home to Fulham before a narrow 1-0 defeat away to Bournemouth in the Area Semi-final.

134

SEASON 1998-99

There was some improvement and a mid-table 12th place was achieved. Two big home defeats were suffered to Wigan and Fulham both 4-0 but otherwise no more than three goals were scored or conceded. In fact scoring three was achieved only four times in the league with no less than thirteen scores of nil. No surprise then that league top scorer Stuart Douglas got only nine and that Phil Gray's five cup goals gave him the highest overall total of just thirteen.

Two players made league debuts notable if only for the fact that in most alphabetical lists of Luton players thay are first and last. Nathaniel 'Tanny' Abbey came through the youth set-up and had made his first team debut with one game in the League Cup the previous season. Goalkeeper Abbey played 68 times for Town before being sold to Chesterfield in 2001 and I remember him as being awful and brilliant pretty much in equal measure. Striker Landry Zahana-Oni was signed from Stirling Albion, was born in Ivory Coast and had played at U17 level for France but played only nine games for Luton before heading back north of the border to Montrose. Signed as a trainee from his local hometown club Aylesbury Athletic, Emmerson Orlando Boyce would play in defence 212 times for the Hatters before moving to Crystal Palace in 2004 and later to Wigan Athletic where he became their Premier League appearance record holder with 263 and skippered the side to an FA Cup Final win against Manchester City, Boyce won 12 caps for Barbados and finished his playing career at Blackpool.

Three players making debuts are worth a mention for very different reasons. Sean Dyche came on loan from Bristol City but is now much more famous for his managerial success at Watford and Burnley. Tresor Kendol was at the time Luton's youngest first team player when he made his debut and was twice voted Young Player of the Year but made only 26 appearances before moving to Cambridge and then Bournemouth. Kendol won one cap for the democratic Republic of Congo but never fulfilled the potential he had shown. Former youth player Michael McIndoe was 18 when he made his debut and had made 49 appearances when his alcohol addition became a problem. Luton met the cost of checking him into The Priory but manager Lennie Lawrence suggested that a fresh start at a new club may also help. This very much proved to be the case, he stayed dry and went on to make 482 league appearances for various clubs and was capped by Scotland B.

There were differing fortunes in the cup competitions. The Auto Windsreens Shield (Associate Members Cup) saw a 3-0 thumping at home to Walsall and in the FA Cup a 3-2 win at Boreham Wood was followed by another home defeat this time at the hands of Hull City 2-1. The League Cup had new sponsors in the shape of Worthington and the Hatters obviously preferred beer to cola as they achieved quite a good run. Aggregate wins against Oxford United 5-4 and Ipswich Town 5-4 were followed by home wins versus Coventry 2-0 and Barnsley 1-0. Defeat finally came in the 5th Round 3-0 away to Sunderland. Off the pitch, the club went into administrative receivership in March 1999 but was able to exit just over six months later on 15th October.

136

On a brighter note, the 1-1 draw against Reading at Kenilworth Road on 3rd March was the setting and inspiration for John Hegley's poem 'A Gray Day'. Any true Hatters fan will identify with it and appreciate the authentic crowd effects. It's on *YouTube* and well worth a look.

SEASON 1999-00

There was very little change in fortunes or in league position, just one place lower at 13th and with only three league fixtures which saw either side score more than three goals. Wins against Oxford United 4-1 and Scunthorpe 4-1 and defeat 4-1 by Bristol Rovers all at Kenilworth Road. There was however a change of sponsor to *SKF* and orange shirts were back with blue trim and blue shorts. Previously known as Skefko Ball Bearing Co. Ltd. the Swedish company had had a factory in Luton since 1911. Top scorer was Liam George with 14 league and 2 cup goals followed by Phil Gray with twelve. There was no money for big signings (or even small ones) and defender Adam Locke came typically on a free transfer from Bristol City making 74 appearances and centre-back Julian Watts came from the same club and made 87 appearances before leaving in 2001 to play for Northern Spirit in Australia. Efetobore 'Efe' Sodje, brother of fellow professionals Sam and Akpo played in only 14 games before he moved on to Crewe and to winning 12 caps for Nigeria including playing in the 2002 World Cup finals. Goalkeeper Ben Roberts shared keeping duties with Tanny Abbey in the first of two loan spells at Luton. When he retired from playing he went to University and gained a First Class Honours degree in Sports Science winning a national award for his dissertation entitled, '*A Bio-mechanical Analysis of a Football Goalkeeper's Jumping Technique*'.

He became goalkeeping coach at three of his former clubs the most recent being Brighton.

Making his debut in midfield at the age of just seventeen was Matthew Taylor but he soon made the left wing back position he own and made 146 appearances and scored 17 goals before being sold to Portsmouth and going on to make almost 500 more appearances there and at Bolton, West Ham and Burnley. There were exits at the first time of asking in both the Worthington (League) Cup 4-2 on aggregate to Bristol Rovers and in the Auto Windscreens Shield (Associate Members Cup) 2-0 away at Oxford. There was a mini-run in the FA Cup with a home win against Kingstonian 4-2 and a 2-2 draw with Lincoln City at Kenilworth Road followed by a 1-0 win in the replay. The 3rd Round also went to a replay but a 2-2 result at Craven Cottage was followed by a 3-0 defeat by Fulham at home.

SEASON 2000-01

The season can be summed up in three words, management merry-go-round mayhem. Lennie Lawrence was sacked on Independence Day 4th July apparently for suggesting that Division 2 (third tier) was Luton's rightful place. Within a week playing legend Ricky Hill was appointed but was dismissed on 15th November having won only two league games. Hill's assistant Lil Fuccillo, another former player was given the job on a caretaker basis. On 7th February 2001 the new manager was announced as former Spurs player Joe Kinnear who had won 26 Republic of Ireland caps.

He had managed the national teams of India and Nepal and more recently had taken Wimbledon as high as 6th place in the Premier League between 1992 and 1999 when he left following a heart attack. He had made a recovery but couldn't do the same for Luton and the season ended with 22nd place and relegation to Division 3 (fourth tier). With a procession of managers there was inevitable musical chairs with players and seventeen made their Luton debuts during this dire season with ten of them playing fewer than fifteen times in their Luton career before moving on. One thing stayed constant, the shirt sponsor was still *SKF* and they were still made by *Olympic Sport* but they had gone back to white with black trim and collar worn with black shorts with white and orange trim.

Some new players were very forgetable but some at least had a touch of the exotic, Freidrich Breitenfelder came from Austria, made 5 appearances and was never heard of again. Kent Karlsen was signed from Oslo, played 9 times and went straight back to Norway. Rocky Baptiste despite the name was from non-league football in London and went back to that after just three appearances. Petri Helin from Finland did stay around long enough to play 27 times and win one of his 27 Finish caps playing against England before leaving for Stockport. Less exotically, former hero Mark Stein came back from Bournemouth for the season but scored only three goals in 36 appearances before moving on to Dagenham & Redbridge. Lee Nogan brother of former player Kurt came in from Darlington but played only seven league games before being moved on to York City. Mark Ovendale came from Bournemouth as stand-in goalkeeper for two seasons then moving to Barry Town before he bacame another cancer victim aged just thirtyseven.

Another goalkeeper worth a mention is Scott Ward who signed for Luton as a seventeen year old. He made his one and only Luton appearance coming on as a substitute and with his very first touch of the ball in league football saved a penalty against Brentford. It was to be his only experience at this level as the remainder of his career was in non-league football.

Two of the debutants would make an impression, one a big one. Peter Holmes was signed from Sheffield Wednesday where he had been a youth player but never got a senior game and would go on to 127 appearances and 12 goals mainly from the left wing before leaving in 2007. The other signed from Northampton Town was a real Luton legend Steve Howard. In just 228 games he would score 103 goals overall and with 96 league goals he is in 4th place in the list of top Luton scorers behind only Gordon Turner, Andy Rennie and Brian Stein. After helping Luton to two promotions, Howard was sold to Derby County in 2006 for £1million and later moved to Leicester City for £1.5million. In the FA Cup progress was actually made to the 3rd Round with Rushden & Diamonds beaten 1-0 at Kenilworth Road and a 0-0 draw at Darlington followed by a 2-0 home win in the replay. Also at home was a 3-3 draw with Queens Park Rangers but there was a 2-1 defeat in the replay at Loftus Road . The Worthington (League) Cup saw an aggregate win over Peterborough before defeat on aggregate 5-1 to Sunderland. Peterborough were again Town's opponents in the Associate Members Cup which now had new sponsors and was known as the LDV Vans Trophy. Posh got their revenge winning 1-0 at London Road.

SEASON 2001-02

Luton bounced straight back with promotion but despite a run of thirteen wins and a draw in the last fourteen games they couldn't catch champions Plymouth Argyle and had to settle for 2nd place. Despite 4-1 defeats at both Mansfield and Macclesfield there were some good away wins at Halifax 4-2, Kidderminster Harriers 4-1 and Hull 4-0 to go with home wins versus Torquay 5-1, Darlington 5-2, Halifax again 5-0 and revenge against Mansfield 5-3. Steve Howard started to build his reputation and respect from the fans with 24 goals from 42 starts backed up by newcomer Dean Crowe with 15 and Matthew Taylor with eleven.

The squad had been strengthened with Carl Emberson who had previously made over 200 league appearances for Colchester coming in from Walsall to take on the bulk of the goalkeeping duties in the two seasons he was at the club. Defender Russell Perrett was signed from Cardiff City and would make109 appearances overall but fall just short with 99 in the league. Jean-Louis Valois was bought from Lille, scored a brilliant goal on his debut but fell out with manager Joe Kinnear and stayed just one season. Dean Crowe was signed from Stoke but after his excellent start he fell away and hampered by a broken leg made only 79 appearances and was loaned to York City before leaving for Oldham in 2004.

There were three signings however who would all make double century status and possibly all qualify as legends. Croatian midfielder and former Yugoslav international Ahmet Brkovic was signed from Leyton Orient and would make 223 appearances and score 38 goals before departing for Millwall in 2008.

141

Defender Chris Coyne came in from Dundee and would spend seven seasons at Kenilworth Road making 252 appearances before leaving for Colchester in 2008 and winning 7 Australian caps. Certain legend is Kevin Nicholls the midfielder signed from Wigan to play the first of his two spells with the Hatters. Nicholls captained Luton to two promotions and a Wembley win in 2009, often playing through the pain of injury he was a huge inspiration to the team. Thirtyfive players were used but the backbone of the team in this promotion year, all making 40 or more appearances were Steve Howard, Kevin Nicholls, Matthew Spring and Matthew Taylor but not forgetting super-sub Adrian Forbes, signed from Norwich with 25 of his 40 appearances being from the substitutes bench but still scoring four goals. Luton were obviously 'concentrating on the league' as being drawn away in all three competitions, they lost the lot. Going down 3-2 to Southend in the FA Cup, 4-0 to Reading in the Worthington (League) Cup and 3-2 to Dagenham & Redbridge in the LDV Vans Trophy.

SEASON 2002-03

There was a fairly solid season back in Division 2 (third tier) with a 9th place finish despite two poor results losing 5-2 away at Blackpool and 4-0 at home to Crewe. These were just about offset by a 5-0 home win against Colchester with the help of a Steve Howard hat-trick. Howard top scored with 22 goals from 41 league games ably assisted by Tony Thorpe on thirteen. Thorpe was back at the club for the fourth time having had brief loan spells from Bristol City in 1998 and 1999 but this time stayed all season before moving on to Queens Park Rangers. The finish was also despite using no less than forty players in the season including an incredible six goalkeepers.

Carl Emberson and Mark Ovendale were joined by new signing Rob Beckwith, Ben Roberts for his second loan spell, this time from Charlton, Cedric Berthelin on loan from Lens and Lars Hirschfeld on loan from Spurs. Hirschfeld played just five games and after very briel spells at Dundee and Leicester moved to Norway and won 48 caps for Canada. Fifteen players made their Luton debut and eight of these including the last two goalkeepers never made it into double figures in terms of appearances. One of these was former youth player Parys Okai who made only four senior appearances, was released to non-league football and died agaed 28 from a drugs overdose at a Halloween event at Leicester in 2013.

There were however three debuts that would prove to be significant. Kevin Foley. Luton born of Irish parents came through the trainee system and would make 166 appearances in defensive midfield before departing for Wolves in 2007 where he would play in over 200 games and win eight Republic of Ireland caps. Stephen Robinson was signed from Preston North End but had already made over 250 appearances for Bournemouth and would make 211 more for Luton in various positions and win two of his seven Northern Ireland caps while at Kenilworth Road where he ended his playing career. Also in Luton legend territory was Sol Davis who was signed from Swindon and who would play in defence 229 times up to 2009. On 28th October 2006, Davis suffered a stroke while travelling to a match at Ipswich. He was taken off the coach and admitted as an emergency at Addenbrooke's Hospital, Cambridge but remarkably was back in the starting line-up for Luton's match at Cardiff on 1st January 2007.

In the FA Cup there was victory 4-0 at home to Guisley before a 3-0 defeat away to Wigan Athletic and in the Worthington (League) Cup a satisfying 2-1 win at Vicarage Road, Watford was followed by exit 3-0 at Villa Park. The LDV Vans Trophy (Associate Members Cup) saw away wins at Woking 2-0 and Stevenage Borough 4-3 before a 2-1 loss to Cambridge at the Abbey Stadium.

SEASON 2003-04

There was off-pitch chaos before the season started when a 'mystery consortium' took over the club and sacked manager Joe Kinnear. Their method of replacing him (or not as the case may be) was to set up a premium rate telephone poll by which players, fans and anyone with cash to spare could vote for either Joe Kinnear, former player Mike Newell or Steve Cotterill who at this stage in his management career had left Cheltenham and Stoke but not yet got to Burnley. After the poll which many thought made the club a laughing stock, it was announced that Mike Newell had won by just four votes. All the players are said to have voted for Kinnear who it was rumoured had actually won the vote but refused to work with the consortium led by businessman John Gurney who had bought the club for just £4. The Football League were not satisfied with the financial arrangements put in place by the consortium and imposed a transfer embargo.The supporters group Trust In Luton became shareholders of one of the club's creditors and with players and staff not having been paid for two months the Trust were able to force the club into Administrative Receivership on 14th July and remove John Gurney after less than two months in charge. Some years later Gurney was declared bankrupt.

After the dust had settled, Kinnear's assistant Mick Harford who had been sacked with him, came back to join his former team mate Newell as Director of Football.

On the pitch the results were fairly good given all the problems off it and a comfortable 10th place in the league was achieved. Yet another kit change saw white shirts with black shoulders and black shorts made by *Xara* and with the new sponsor *Travel Extras*. There were just three nasty defeats all away at Brentford 4-2, Bournemouth 6-3 and Hartlepool 4-3 but there was revenge against Brentford with a 4-1 win at Kenilworth Road. Steve Howard top scored again with 16 and loanee Gary McSheffrey from Coventry scored 9. In 1999 McSheffrey had been the youngest player to appear in the Premier League and would go on to a succesful career at Coventry and elsewhere. There were again problems in goal but this time only four keepers were used. Rob Beckwith played the first third of the season and was then injured which allowed Marlon Beresford to come in from Bradford City despite the transfer embargo. Once this was lifted Beresford, who had played 240 league games for Burnley, was able to make the transfer permanent, make 132 appearances and become a crowd favourite. The latter part of the season was covered by Danish U21 international goalie Morten Hyldgaard who then retired and Luton born 18 year old Dean Brill had come on as a substitute for Beckwith, played four more games and eventually made 109 appearances in his two spells at the club.

Other debutants included Enoch Showunmi who played up front in the second part of the season and would play 114 times scoring 16 goals and winning two caps for Nigeria before leaving for Bristol City in 2006.

Two players coming through from the youth team were one who would go on to greater things and another who would become yet another Luton legend. Curtis Davies played just 62 times in defence before being sold for £3million and making a name for himself in the upper levels at West Bromwich, Aston Villa, Birmingham City, Hull City and Derby County. Luton born Keith Keane another defender made his debut aged just sixteen and would go on to make 285 appearances in defence and midfield. He won four Ireland U21 caps and for many was man of the match when Luton won at Wembley in 2009.

Signed the previous season from Grimsby Town but making his debut this was Welsh international defender Alan Neilson who would play no more than 63 times but would later serve on the coaching staff under five managers and would be called on three times to act as caretaker manager. The League Cup had changed beer sponsors and was now the Carling Cup in which Luton scored eight goals in two ties but still went out. A 4-1 win at home against Yeovil but a 4-4 extra time draw away at Charlton was settled on penalties with Town losing 8-7. The LDV Vans Trophy gave the Hatters three away ties with wins at Stevenage Borough 1-0 and Rushden & Diamonds 2-1 followed by defeat 3-0 at Southend. The best run was in the FA Cup, there was a 3-1 replay win at home to Thurrock after 1-1 away and away wins at Rochdale 2-0 and Bradford City 2-1 but defeat came in the 4th Round by a single goal at home to Tranmere Rovers.

SEASON 2004-05

Luton ended the previous season in 'New' Football League Division Two but started this one in English Football League One but still in the third tier. The 'New' Football League Division One was now known as The Championship and by the end of the season the Hatters would be promoted to it. The club had finally come out of Administrative Receivership on 24th May but little money was available for new signings which was possibly a blessing as the result was a very settled team. There were just six debuts including striker Calvin Andrew, Luton born youth player who had little influence this season but would clock up 67 appearances before moving to Crystal Palace in 2008. Slovenian goalkeeper Dino Seremet covered for Marlon Beresford when he was injured and Warren Feeney was signed from Stockport and played a few games at the end of the season. He would go on to make 83 appearances, score eleven goals and win fifteen of his 46 Northern Ireland caps while at the club. The most influential in this promotion season was Rowan Vine on loan from Portsmouth for the whole season, virtually ever-present and a great goal provider with numerous assists. Vine's move was later made permanent for £250,000, he scored 33 goals in 111 matches and was sold to Birmingham City in 2007 for £2.5million.

Seven players appeared in 40 or more league games, Ahmet Brkovic (15 goals), Chris Coyne, Curtis Davies, Sol Davis, Steve Howard (18 goals), Kevin Nicholls (12 goals) and Rowan Vine. Add to this Kevin Foley (39), Marlon Beresford (38), Paul Underwood (37) and super-sub Enoch Showunmi (35 appearances including 28 from the bench) and you have a remarkably stable team.

This led to some great results including home wins versus Bradford 4-0, Wrexham 5-1, Bristol City 5-0 and Brentford 4-2 and good away wins at Barnsley 4-3, Milton Keynes 4-1 and Torquay 4-1. The championship was won with two games to spare and a run of sixteen wins, eight draws and only two losses from 21st December gave Luton top spot twelve points clear of second place Hull City. League success was not matched in the cups with defeat 2-0 at Swansea in the LDV Vans Trophy and a 4-3 loss to Boston United away in the Carling (League) Cup. In the FA Cup there were away wins against Southend 3-0 and Wycombe Wanderers by the same score with Steve Howard scoring two in both games taking his season tally to 22 but the run ended with Brentford winning 2-0 at Kenilworth Road.

SEASON 2005-06

There was a solid start in the new Championship and a 10th place finish out of 24 with some good performances including home wins against Norwich 4-2 and Crewe 4-1 but there were also some hard games away from home including defeats at Sheffield United 4-0 and Preston 5-1.Top goals scorers in the league were again Steve Howard with 14 and Rowan Vine with 10 from only 31 games due to early season injury. In September a large number of former players gathered to celebrate 100 years at Kenilworth Road including Mike Cullen, Mike Keen, Terry Branston, John Moore, Kirk Stephens, Alan West, Julian James, Kingsley Black, Wally Shanks and 1959 cup finalists Ron Baynham, Dave Pacey, Billy Bingham, Seamus Dunne, Ken Hawkes and Tony Gregory. In that same month there was less for fans to celebrate when Luton sold Curtis Davies to West Bromwich Albion for £3million, a new Luton record.

148

A new sponsor had also been found and *Electrolux* had their name on white shirts with orange and black trim and black shorts made by *Diadora*. Electrolux had been manufacturing electrical appliances in Luton since 1927.Most of the players who had featured heavily in the previous season did so again and were joined by three of the new signings. Central defender Markus 'Mako' Heikkinen was signed from Aberdeen and would make 77 appearances and win eleven of his 61 caps for Finland before moving to Rapid Wien (Vienna) in 2007 and making 170 league appearances there. Defender/winger Carlos Edwards came from Wrexham and would make 74 appearances, score eight goals, win 19 of his 90 caps for Trinidad & Tobago and play against England in the 2006 World Cup before he was sold to Sunderland for £1.5million also in 2007.

Wide player Dean Morgan signed from Reading would feature in 101 matches before a number of loan spells at various clubs and final departure in 2009. Another debutant who would feature more in the future was David Bell from Rushden & Diamonds. The Carling (League) Cup saw two away ties, a 3-1 win at Leyton Orient and a 1-0 defeat at Reading. In Round 3 of the FA Cup there was defeat at home against Liverpool but a classic which I remember so well watching on TV. Liverpool opened the scoring through Steven Gerrard but Luton were deservedly level through Steve Howard, who should have scored earlier. Mako Heikkinen had a header cleared off the line and then a lovely through ball from Carlos Edwards enabled Steve Robinson to take Carragher out of the game and rifle the ball into the net just two minutes before half time. After the break the Reds should have been level with a penalty but Cisse's effort was saved by Marlon Beresford.

Three minutes later Kevin Nicholls showed Cisse how to do it after a foul in the box on Rowan Vine and Luton were 3-1 up. Liverpool brought on Pongolle who almost immediately scored in the 62nd minute, less than ten minutes later Alonso equalized from 40 yards with a shot that seemed to change direction at least twice before going past Beresford. Liverpool took the lead when Pongolle nodded in a cross and in the 90th minute Beresford went up for a Luton corner in search of the equalizer. Liverpool scrambled it clear to Alonso who from well inside his own half thumped the ball towards and in slow motion into Luton's net. Travesty!

SEASON 2006-07

It all started so well, in October a 5-1 win against Leeds United at Kenilworth Road put Luton in 5th place in the Championship but that win was followed by seven straight defeats and then only three wins In the period up to 15th March 2007 when manager Mike Newell was finally sacked. Former player Brian Stein was made caretaker until the appointment of former Leeds manager Kevin Blackwell just under two weeks later. Blackwell had kept goal for several league clubs over a twenty year playing career, was Luton born but was no a miracle worker and achieved only one win and one draw before the final humiliation of a 5-0 home defeat by Sunderland in the last game of the season. Blackwell's only consolation could be that Leeds United, the club that had sacked him were one place lower and also relegated.

It was hardly a surprise with goalscorers Steve Howard and Kevin Nicholls gone pre-season, Rowan Vine sold to Birmingham for £2.5million in mid-season (but still being top scorer with 12 from 26 games) and Carlos Edwards sold to Sunderland in January. Luton were severely restricted financially and so a number of players came in on short term loans including Clarke Carlisle from Watford who would achiieve fame as Chairman of the PFA Management Committee and later attempt suicide with mental health problems. Austrian Besian Idrizaj came from Liverpool for seven games and he would die in 2010 aged 22 from a suspected heart attack in his sleep. Irish international goalkeeper Dean Kiely was borrowed from Portsmouth for 11 games and Swedish U21 international Bjorn Runstrom came from Fulham for just eight appearances.

Other debutants enjoyed varying degrees of success. Striker Adam Boyd was signed from Hartlepool on a three year contract for £500,000 but managed just two goals in 23 appearances and was released after one season. Jamaican international midfielder Richard Langley came from QPR, scored a single goal in 34 appearances, many as substitute and also lasted a single season. Drew Talbot came in from Sheffield Wednesday and made 65 appearances before leaving for Chesterfield in 2009. Sam Parkin was signed from Ipswich and was another who played just one season before being sent out for a season on loan but he was back to take part at Wembley in 2009. Another who stayed long enough to be a member of the Wembley team was Lewis Emanuel signed from Bradford City and making 88 appearances before being released in 2010. Three years later he was sent to prison for eight years for robbing a post office in York with an imitation firearm.

In the FA Cup there was a replay win 1-0 against Queens Park Rangers after a 2-2 draw at Loftus Road but this was followed by a 4-0 demolition at home by Blackburn Rovers. There were three away ties in the Carling (League) Cup with a win on penalties after 1-1 after extra time against Bristol Rovers, a 3-0 win versus Brentford but another 4-0 hammering this time by Everton at Goodison Park.

SEASON 2007-08

Manager Blackwell decided that what was needed was 'experience' so he sold Leon Barnett, Kevin Foley and Russ Perrett, let Mako Heikkinen go on free transfer and released Adam Boyd one year into a three year contract that had cost £500,000. He then signed a string of players who by the end of the season would have retired or gone on to lesser things. Striker Paul Furlong from QPR was 38 years old and contributed eight goals in 32 appearances. Scottish international Don Hutchison played 26 times and retired. Canadian international Paul Peschisolido released by Derby made two starts and came off the bench three times before injury finished his career, he was famously married to Karren Brady of Birmingham City and TV's *The Apprentice* and later managed Burton Albion.

In fairness to Hutchison, when released he refused his last two pay packets to sponsor two youth team players and in fairness to Blackwell, the club was in dire straights financially.

Other new signings who at least played thirty or more games before departing included defenders Alan Goodall from Rochdale, Richard Jackson from Derby, Darren Currie nephew of England player Tony Currie from Ipswich and Chris Perry, who Spurs once paid £4million for, came from West Bromwich.

Midfielder Paul McVeigh from Norwich City did at least stay until 2009 and make 53 appearances before going back to the Canaries. On Boxing Day at Bristol Rovers I did see one memorable game. Chris Coyne was sent off after fifteen minutes and Rovers scored from the resultant penalty, five minutes before the break Robinson was shown his second yellow and went too. In the second half the nine men equalized only for Grant to be shown a straight red for an awful tackle with about 15 minutes to go. Somehow the eight held on and even Rovers 'Gasheads' applauded at the end.

The result of all this 'experience' was that they all experienced a disastrous season and had the experience of finishing bottom and succesive relegations. The club had been placed into receivership for the third time in November 2007 and this meant an automatic ten point deduction but even without this the Hatters would have gone down. In January Kevin Blackwell gave a months notice of leaving the club but was sacked three weeks before that notice ran out and the job was given to old favourite Mick Harford but there was nothing he could do to prevent the inevitable. One thing he did do in the last match of the season was to bring a 17 year-old off the bench to make his debut. That teenager was Jake Howells who by 2012 with 183 appearances under his belt became Luton's longest serving player. He made his 250th appearance aged 22 and his 300th aged just twentythree.

By the time he made his last appearance and went on loan to Yeovil Town his final tally was 334 and 31 goals, certainly another legend. Despite dire league form, there were some reasonable cup performances. The Johnstone's Paint Trophy (Associate Members Cup) saw a 2-0 home win against Northampton Town before defeat 4-3 away at Gillingham. In the FA Cup a 2-0 replay win against Brentford away followed a 1-1 draw at Kenilworth Road where Nottingham Forest were beaten 1-0 and Liverpool held to another 1-1 before a crushing 5-0 exit at Anfield. The Carling (League) Cup saw a 2-1 away win at Dagenham & Redbridge and then three home ties with wins against Sunderland 3-0 and Charlton 3-1 before a narrow defeat by Everton 1-0. On 26th February there had finally been a move in the right direction financially when control of the club was assumed by LTFC2020 a consortium of businessmen who were fans of the club including League Cup hero Steve Foster and headed by TV presenter Nick Owen.

SEASON 2008-09

Pre-season the FA imposed a penalty of ten points for 'financial irregularities' then on 10th July the FA joined in and deducted twenty points for 'Exiting administration without an agreed CVA in place'.(A Company Voluntary Agreement is a legally binding document under which creditors receive an agreed proportion of debt repaid over a period of time). To every fan it seemed totally unjust that they and the club were being punished for the misdeeds of those long gone. So a totally surreal season began with Luton bottom of the table on minus 30 points before a ball had been kicked and with enough new players, mostly on free transfers and loans, to field two teams The team they did field for the first game included an incredible eight debutants.

154

Some new signings went on to make valuable contributions in this season and beyond. Defender George Pilkington came from Port Vale and would make 172 appearances and become club captain. French midfielder/winger Claude Gnapka (Johouri) came in from Peterborough and would score 27 goals (one very important) in 136 appearances before moving to Walsall. Asa Hall signed from Birmingham played 89 times and Rossi Jarvis from Norwich 77 times but both fell out of favour when Mick Harford left the club. Fellow Norwich players striker Chris Martin and defender Micky Spillane played virtually every game in their one season. Martin went on to play 150 plus games for Derby County and win 17 caps for Scotland. Striker Tom Craddock signed from Middlesborough originally on loan and scored 38 goals in just 86 appearances and former QPR star Kevin Gallen netted 21 times in 75 games. Despite all this new firepower, Paul Furlong and Matt Spring were joint top scorers with 12 each in all competitions. Another debutant lasting only one season was shirt manufacturer and sponsor *Carbrini*, a sportswear company owned by JD Sports. Their shirts were white with blue and orange trim with blue shorts with orange and white trim.

Other newcomers had little impact, few less than Josh Klein-Davies on loan from Bristol Rovers and hot from a loan spell at Yate Town. He came on as a substitute in the first game of the season, a 3-1 loss to Port Vale at Kenilworth Road. He was never picked again and his subsequent career saw him playing for just about every club that exists within a thirty mile radius of Bristol including Almondsbury Town. Another at least scored a goal in his five appearances and is worth a mention just for his name, Sunday-Akanni Wasiu on loan from Colchester.

On January 13th a 2-2 draw at Chester saw the Hatters reach the milestone of zero points but the inevitable end came when Luton lost the last six games of the season and ended relegated from the Football League in 24th place. Even with those six losses they would have been comfortably in mid-table without the deductions. In the FA Cup two games against Altrincham failed to produce a goal and after extra time in the away replay Luton won 4-2 on penalties only to be beaten 3-1 by Southend at Roots Hall in Round 2. In the Carling (League) Cup there was a home win against Plymouth Argyle 2-0 followed by a 5-1 thrashing by Reading at the Madejski Stadium.

The Johnstone's Paint Trophy provided all the drama. Entering the competition in Round 2 Luton needed a 4-3 penalty shoot-out win after a 2-2 draw with Brentford at Kenilworth Road. Next was a 1-0 win away at Walsall before a home win 1-0 in the Area Semi-Final versus Colchester. The Area Final was over two legs against Brighton & Hove Albion and with 0-0 away and 1-1 home it was penalties again and another 4-3 win. The Final was at Wembley against Scunthorpe United who were a division higher and was played in front of 55,378 fans of which at least 40,000 were supporting Luton and were determined to let the FA and FL know exactly what they thought of points deductions. Scunthorpe opened the scoring through Hooper after 14 minutes which was equalised by Chris Martin after just over half an hour. Tom Craddock scored on 70 minutes to give Town the lead and it stayed that way until the 88th minute when McCann put the sides level and took the game into extra time. Substitute Claude Gnapka scored just five minutes in to start what seemed a very long half hour. It was a bitter-sweet moment as I stood with my brother and watched Kevin Nicholls on his return to the club lift the trophy.

My team had won a trophy, this time at the new Wembley Stadium but non-league Conference football next season was virtually certain. The team that won that trophy was Dean Brill, Michael Spillane, Lewis Emanuel, Keith Keane, Ed Asafu-Adjaye, George Pilkington, Rossi Jarvis, Kevin Nicholls, Tom Craddock, Asa Hall and Chris Martin with substitutes used Claude Gnapka and Sam Parkin.(Jake Howells who played in every round except the final was given a medal). When relegation did become a certainty, Luton made a request that they should be able to defend the trophy – needless to say the Football League refused.

SEASON 2009-10

Luton were back in non-league football for the first time since 1920 and even I was not old enough to remember that. So a new season and some very different venues, Forest Green Rovers played only a few miles from my home and ran a vegetarian stadium on green energy so it was take your own pies. Kidderminster on the other hand offered generous portions of really tasty shepherds pie from vast vats of the stuff. Orange shirts were back again still made by *Carbrini* but now sponsored jointly by *Easy Jet* and *NICEIC*.This was the local touch again with Easy Jet based at Luton Airport and the National Inspection Council for Electrical Installation Contracting having its HQ in my birthplace, Houghton Regis. Shorts were white but would change to blue when *Fila* took over manufacture. Despite a start of six wins and three draws in the first twelve games, Mick Harford left the club 'by mutual consent' on 1st October. Coach Alan Neilson acted as caretaker until the appointment of yet another former Luton player Richard Money (aka Dickie Dosh).

Money had previously managed Walsall having started his mangement career at Scunthorpe and also managed in Sweden and Australia.

Goals were not a problem and the Hatters scored four four times and six three times – home to Greys Athletic 6-0 and Histon 6-3 and notably away at Ebbsfleet United 6-1 when all six were in the second half with a Claude Gnapka hat-trick. Just for a change, in the 8-0 demolition of Hayes & Yeading at Kenilworth Road, seven came in the first half. Top scorers were Tom Craddock with 24 and Kevin Gallen with 18

Once again there had been a large turnover of players with some worthy of note amongst them. Matthew Barnes-Homer came from Kidderminster Harriers and would score 23 goals from 81 appearances before departing in 2011. Luton born defender Shane Blackett was signed from Peterborough but his appearances were restricted by injuries to just 51. Hungarian defender Janos Kovacs came in from Lincoln City in the first of his two spells at the club that would see him play 91 times. Alan White came back to Kenilworth Road for a second time and would take his appearances up to 110. Goalkeeper Kevin Pilkington was signed from Notts County but the keeper who would soon attain legend status was Mark Tyler who had made over 400 appearances for Peterborough. He quickly became a hero with some early penalty saves and would play 297 times between the sticks before returning to Peterborough as player/coach in 2016.In 2013-14 Tyler set a club record with 23 clean sheets. Now playing in the lowly FA Trophy, there was a 1st Round exit 3-1 away to Cambridge United but something of a run in the FA Cup despite starting in the unfamiliar regions of the qualifying rounds.

Grays Athletic were beaten 3-0 at Kenilworth Road where Luton then drew 3-3 with Rochdale winning the replay 2-0. It took another replay to get past Rotherham United 3-0 after a 2-2 draw away but the end came at Southampton with a narrow 1-0 defeat.

Town had finished 2nd in the Blue Square Bet Conference but only first place got automatic promotion, Stevenage Borough (who dropped Borough from their name to celebrate).The next four went into play-offs which was wonderful if you were York City who had finished fifth but not so wonderful for runners-up who would have been automatically promoted if play-offs didn't exist. Even less wonderful were the semi-final scores, York 1 Luton 0 in both legs. So Luton were condemned to another non-league season along with York who had lost to Oxford United in the play-off final.

SEASON 2010-11

Another good campaign was enjoyed by the fans with home wins including Forest Green Rovers 6-1, Histon 5-1, Darlington 4-0, Southport 6-0 and the most satisfying being some sort of play-off revenge, York City 5-0. Histon were also beaten 4-0 away. Top scorers were Matthew Barnes-Homer with 20 and Claude Gnapka with 15. On 28th March with Luton third in the table, Richard Money left the club and was replaced by his assistant Gary Brabin. Money had been confrontational with fans, critical of players and had never been popular despite having the best win ratio of any Luton manager. Once again there had been a massive turnover of players with well over twenty making their debut.

159

Five are worthy of note including Zdenek Kroca imported from the Czech Republic who was well used in his one season with Town making 55 appearances and scoring 7 goals. Two players both signed from Cambridge United were Robbie Willmott who would play 67 times and score 15 goals and Danny Crow with 17 goals in 70 appearances. Most influential would be Alex Lawless signed from York who would make 203 appearances and contribute 22 goals before departing for Yeovil Town in 2016. Striker Amari Morgan-Smith from Ilkeston was productive with 18 goals from just 48 games, There was also a debut for midfielder JJ O'Donnell whose career was thought to be finished when he became the first professional footballer to suffer from sesamoiditis (severe inflamation of bones beneath the big toe). The club and fans helped to fund numerous operations and he was released to become kit man at Gateshead. After more painful treatment and two and a half years he was eventually able to play again for that club.

In the FA Cup St Albans City were disposed of 4-0 at Kenilworth Road but the Hatters were held 1-1 at Corby Town before a 4-2 replay win. There was another replay in the 2nd Round when a 2-2 draw against Charlton at The Valley was followed by exit 3-1 at home. There was better fortune in the FA Trophy with almost a place in the final. Welling United held Town to a 0-0 draw at Kenilworth Road but were beaten 2-1 on their ground. Then came home wins against Uxbridge 4-0 and Gloucester City 1-0 and an away win 1-0 at Guisley. The semi-final over two legs was against Mansfield Town who took a one goal lead into the second leg at Kenilworth Road. Luton scored and the scores were level at full time with The Stags getting the winner in extra time.

Then came the serious stuff, third place in the league had given the joy of another play-off place. This time there was no mistake in the semi-finals and Wrexham were beaten 3-0 away and 2-1 at home for a place in the final against AFC Wimbledon. For some unknown reason the Final took place in the City of Manchester Stadium and it was no surprise that the attendance was just over 18,000 to see two southern clubs. The previous four finals had all been at Wembley with crowds all over 40,000 and every final since has been at Wembley.The game itself was a great disappointment with a 0-0 scoreline at full time. Luton had one really good chance to win it in extra time but the shot went wide and it was down to penalties. Wimbledon's Kaid Mohamed and Alex Lawless both missed one and it was Jason Walker whose weak chip was saved to condemn Luton to another season of non-league football. It was Walker's last game for Luton and it was a very long drive home with my brother from Manchester.

SEASON 2011-12

There was a good start to the season and obviously a liking for clubs from the North with 5-1 wins at Kenilworth Road against Southport, Barrow and Gateshead. Kettering didn't enjoy their holiday as the Hatters beat them 5-0 home and away on Boxing Day and New Years Day. There had been an unbeaten run in the first ten games of the season but form began to dip in the new year and as a result manager Gary Brabin was sacked on 31st March.to be replaced just over a week later by Paul Buckle.

161

Buckle seemed a strange choice, he had achieved some success at Torquay United but more recently taken over at relegated Bristol Rovers where he had got rid of virtually the whole of the squad he inherited, brought in nineteen new players, become universally hated by the fans and was sacked as the team seemed bound for another relegation. In fairness, he did halt the mini-slide, get Luton into 5th place and yet again, the play-offs. Due partly to the management change an incredible 45 players were used in the season, almost half of these making debuts and nine playing fewer than ten games. Of the newcomers only two rate a mention, Stuart Fleetwood was signed from Hereford United and would go on to score 27 goals in 88 appearances and was top scorer this season with sixteen.

The other significant newcomer was signed by Brabin just before his departure, Andre Gray was picked up from Hinckley United (literally under the noses of Leicester City), played the last nine games of the season and scored five goals (one in each of his first four games which was a club record) and would eventually net 57 times in 111 matches. When I saw him for the first time the following season it was obvious that with his skill and particularly pace he was destined for greater things and so it was via Brentford to the Premier League with Burnley and Watford. In the FA Cup Town had three home ties winning against Hendon 5-1 and Northampton Town 1-0 before going out 4-2 to Cheltenham. The FA Trophy took Luton to another semi-final appearance with wins over Swindon Supermarine, Hinckley United (when Andre Gray was first spotted), Kidderminster Harriers and Gateshead before losing 2-1 on aggregate over two legs to York City.

The promotion play-offs brought a semi-final against Wrexham for the second year running and a 3-2 aggregate win thanks to a George Pilkington penalty. So another final against, guess who, York City. I was in the USA on match day and wore a Luton shirt much to the bemusement of Nashville residents and amusement of some of my fellow holidaymakers but it failed to work and despite an early Andre Gray goal, our nemesis won 2-1.

SEASON 2012-13

Another season in the Blue Square Bet Conference was made even harder to take by virtue of the fact that the previous three champions Stevenage, Crawley Town and Fleetwood Town had never been in the Football League before. Once again there was an influx of players on loans or short term contracts but there were a good number who stayed at least a full season and four who would have a big impact on the club's future, particularly in the following season. Defender Ronnie Henry was signed from Stevenage and would spend two seasons as club captain and make 87 appearances before returning to Stevenage. I remember his grandfather Ron as full-back in the famous double winning Spurs team of the 1960s. Ron senior played over 250 times for Tottenham, won an England cap and fortunately lived just long enough to see his grandson lift the Conference Premier champions trophy for Luton in 2014. Defender Scott Griffiths was signed from Peterborough and would make 115 appearances. Midfielder Jonathan Smith came from York City initially on loan and would make 176 appearances in the Luton shirt.

Last but by no means least was central defender Steve McNulty signed from Fleetwood Town who made 125 appearances and succeeded Ronnie Henry as club captain before being allowed to move to Tranmere for family reasons.

Macca with his prematurely grey hair was 6'1" but looked shorter (possibly due to his width), never seemed to jump very high but rarely missed a defensive header, was a good passer of the ball along the ground and always led by example. It was good to see him captain Tranmere Rovers to victory and back to the Football League in the 2018 play-off final. Highlights at Kenilworth Road were wins against Macclesfield 4-1 and Barrow 6-1 with a Jon Shaw hat-trick but travelling supporters had to endure defeats at Grimsby 4-1, Newport County 5-2 and Gateshead 5-1, Top scorer was Andre Gray with 20 followed by Stuart Fleetwood on eleven.

In the FA Trophy Luton overcame Dorchester Town 3-1 in a replay after a 2-2 away draw, Matlock Town 2-1 away and Skelmersdale United 2-0 at home before a 3-0 defeat to Grimsby Town at Blundell Park. The real excitement though was in the FA Cup with Cambridge United beaten 2-0 away, Nuneaton Town beaten in an away replay 2-0 after a 1-1 draw at Kenilworth Road and Dorchester Town 2-1 at home (they had to come back again three days later for their FA Trophy defeat). This put the Hatters into Round 3 with the big boys and Championship club Wolverhampton Wanderers were despatched 1-0 at home to give Luton an away tie at top flight Norwich City. No-one gave Town a chance but Scott Rendell scored the only goal of the game at Carrow Road and Luton were the first non-league team ever to beat a Premier League team in the FA Cup.

It couldn't go on for ever and Millwall won 3-0 at Kenilworth Road in the 5th Round. Paul Buckle left the club for 'undisclosed personal reasons' on 19th February. The reasons were a mystery for a long time but it was eventually discovered that his girl friend had landed a TV presenters job in the USA and he wanted to follow her. He came back some time later to manage Cheltenham Town but lasted only 79 days and was last heard of somewhere outside Sacramento. John Still had been at Dagenham & Redbridge for over nine years but was persuaded to take the job. He had got both Dagenham and Maidenhead out of non-league football, he couldn't do it again could he? Despite being unbeaten in the last five games Luton could only manage 7th place. It was almost a relief not to be in the play-offs.

SEASON 2013-14

There were to be no play-offs this season either because this time Luton were crowned Champions with three matches left to play. Manager John Still had brought in players who would help to make this possible and also play a part in coming seasons back in the Football League. Striker Paul Benson who had played for Still at Dagenham & Redbridge was signed from Swindon, initially on a one season loan but he would score 25 goals in 85 appearances before moving back to Dagenham in 2016 but crucially 17 of those goals were scored in this promotion season. Another striker Mark Cullen signed a two year contract when released by Hull City and would score 24 times in 83 games before his £180,000 move to Blackpool in 2015. That move would come back to haunt the Hatters later.

Midfielder Luke Gutteridge came from Northampton Town and would score 19 times in 74 appearances but again 13 of those goals were in this season. Gutteridge fell out of favour when John Still left and followed him to Dagenham & Redbridge. Midfielder Cameron McGeehan was acquired from Norwich City initially on loan and would make 106 appearances and contribute 31 goals before leaving for Barnsley in 2017. Pelly Ruddock Mpanzu came from West Ham United and has clocked up 154 appearances to date and signed a new three year contract in 2017. Elliot Justham came in from East Thurrock United and would be back-up goalkeeper for Mark Tyler for three seasons.

It was a season of records, with 27 league games undefeated between 17th September and 17th March and 15 consecutive away games undefeated. Goalkeeper Mark Tyler kept 23 clean sheets and the championship was won with 101 points which was 19 more than nearest rivals Cambridge United. (Cambridge were also promoted beating Halifax and Gateshead in the play-offs). Then there were goals, goals, goals including home wins against Halifax 4-3, Hyde 4-1, Gateshead 4-2, Forest Green Rovers 4-1, Wrexham 5-0, Kidderminster 6-0 and the best Hereford United 7-0. The Hatters weren't too bad away either with wins including at Woking 4-0, Tamworth 4-3, Alfreton Town 5-0 and Nuneaton 5-0. Andre Gray scored 30, Paul Benson 18 and Luke Gutteridge 13 in all competitions but there were fourteen others who got the ball into the net. In this season of 102 goals I managed to get to four games with my brother at Forest Green Rovers 0-0, Hereford United 0-0, Salisbury City 0-0 and Kidderminster Harriers 2-0, it would have been nice to have seen some of the other one hundred!

Cup football was not a matter of great concern to fans in this historic season which was just as well as in the FA Cup Town struggled past Woking 1-0 away and then lost 2-1 away at Welling United. In the FA Trophy it took a replay to get past Staines Town 2-0 after a 0-0 away draw. Wrexham were beaten 2-0 at Kenilworth Road before a 2-2 away draw was followed by a home replay defeat 1-0 to Cambridge United who would join Luton in EFL 2 next season. But nobody cared.

SEASON 2014-15

There was a solid start back in the Football League (or English Football League as we now had to remember to call it) and 8th place was achieved and could have been better had the Hatters not lost all six matches in March and the first one in April 2015. Goals were much harder to come by, just 43 in the league compared to the previous seasons 102 and Luton did not score more than three in any league game but neither did they concede mor than three. The situation was not helped by the fact that Andre Gray had been sold to Brentford for £500,000 pre-season and Paul Benson broke a leg restricting him to just 21 league appearances. Mark Cullen top scored with just 13 in the league. Here were two notable signings with attacking midfielder Andy Drury, who had previously been at the club in 2010-11, being signed from Crawley Town for £100,000 and making 39 appearances in the season bringing his final tally to 58 with 8 goals. Defender Luke Wilkinson came from Dagenham & Redbridge on a one year deal which was later extended. Virtually ever-present this season he went on to make 72 appearances for Luton.

167

During the campaign Mark Cullen and Steve McNulty both made over 40 appearances and there were large contributions from Jake Howells, Mark Tyler and Scott Griffiths. Tyler and his stand-in Elliot Justham kept seventeen clean sheets between them.

One interesting debutant was Elliot Lee on loan from West Ham who scored three goals in his eleven appearances. He would return to the club in 2017 joining brother Olly and make a big impact. The League Cup was by now sponsored by Capital One but Town's first game back in this competition ended in a home defeat 2-1 to Swindon Town. The Johnstone's Paint Trophy provided no more of a welcome back with a 1-0 defeat at Crawley but there was a mini-run in the FA Cup. Newport County were beaten 4-2 at Kenilworth Road (The only score of more than three all season). This was followed by a 1-1 draw at Bury and a 1-0 replay win before going out 2-1 to Cambridge United at the Abbey Stadium.

SEASON 2015-16

Luton didn't make the progress fans hoped for or indeed expected and went the whole of August without a win. I was at one of those matches at Yeovil which was a classic game of two halves. First half, glorious sunshine, worried about possible sunburn and Town 2-0 up. Second half, literally soaked to the skin on the open terrace before stewards were eventually persuaded to let us into the empty seats under cover to escape the torrential rain and the Glovers scored three times to win the match.Things came to a head with three succesive defeats home to Carlisle 4-3, away at Newport 3-0, (I had the 'pleasure' of watching that one too) and 4-3 to Northampton at Kenilworth Road.

John Still was dismissed by the Board 'with a heavy heart'. He had been made a Freeman of the Borough of Luton, was already a Freeman of the Borough of Barking & Dagenham but will always be remembered as '*The Man who got us Back Into The League*'. He soon returned to his job at Dagenham & Redbridge and literally as I write has been appointed manager of relegated Barnet. Could he possibly do it four times? Academy boss Andy Awford took on the caretaker role until the appointment of Brighton Assistant Manager, Welshman Nathan Jones on 6th January. Jones had been signed by Luton for £10,00 from Merthyr Tydfil in 1995 but made no first team appearances before leaving to play in Spain. On return he made over 450 leaguw appearances mainly for Brighton and Yeovil. Jones took Luton from the threat of relegation to a very safe 11th place by the end of the season. New shirt sponsors were Barnfield College, Bedfordshire's largest further education establishment with two campuses in Luton but still in conjunction with NICEIC.

Alex Wall, Mark Cullen and Alex Lacey had all gone pre-season, Steve McNulty had been allowed to leave for Tranmere after just 10 games for personal family reasons, Luke Gutteridge was released after just eight, Luke Wilkinson moved to Stevenage mid-season and Jake Howells was loaned to Yeovil in October.In the other direction loanee Cameron McGeehan's move was made permanent. Scottish international Craig Mackail-Smith who had played for Still at Dagenham came in from Brighton and would contribute 5 goals in his 40 appearances before being loaned to Peterborough and then transferred to Wycombe Wanderers.

169

Jack Marriot came from Ipswich and scored 28 goals in 91 appearances in his two seasons before his move to Peterborough where he had an even better strike rate of 33 goals in 56 games in 2017-18.

Scott Cuthbert was signed from Leyton Orient, became club captain on the departure of Steve McNulty and clocked up 111 appearances until his recent release. Full back Dan Potts came from West Ham and has made 89 appearances to date. He is the son of former West Ham skipper Steve Potts and has unusually played for both England and USA at U20 level. Midfielder Olly Lee was signed from Birmingham and has made 123 appearances and scored 11 goals including an incredible 65 yard shot against Cambridge United. Olly and his brother Elliot are the sons of Rob Lee of Newcastle and England fame. Terms have been agreed for Olly's move to Hearts.

There was a bonus when Andre Gray was transferred from Brentord to Burnley and it was revealed that a sell-on clause meant that an additional £1.1million would come to Luton with a further £0.7million if Burnley were promoted to the Premier League with Gray in the squad, they were and he was. With all the comings and goings and managerial change only seven players made 30 or more appearances and only two of those made forty or more, fortunately these two were the top scorers Jack Marriot and Cameron McGeeham with thirty goals between them. Luton managed two ties in each of the cup tournaments, in the Johnston's Paint FA Trophy beating beating Leyton Orient 2-1 at home and losing by the same score to Gillingham away. In the FA Cup a 2-1 win away at Crawley Town was followed by defeat 2-0 at London Road, Peterborough.

170

The best performance was in the Capital One (League) Cup when a 3-1 home victory over Bristol City was followed by a 1-1 scoreline against Premier League Stoke City only losing 8-7 on penalties.

SEASON 2016-17

Nathan Jones was not one to hang around and fourteen players left the club pre-season and four more in January. Among those who left were five who had done good things for the club in recent times, striker Paul Benson and goalkeeper Elliot Justham joined up again with John Still at Dagenham & Redbridge. Jake Howells moved to Eastleigh, Alex Lawless to Yeovil Town and Scot Griffiths was released. Ten new players were signed, five of which would play a major role in the season ahead. Striker Danny Hylton and his team mate Johnny Mullins came in from Oxford United, Mullins played 29 times in defence and Hylton top scored with 27 goals from 47 appearances. Defender Glen Rea came in from Brighton, was virtually ever-present and has now taken his appearances over 100. Fellow defender Alan Sheeham from Bradford City has also become a centurion in terms of appearances and a very useful free kick specialist as well. Isaac Vassell came from Truro City and scored 14 goals in 53 games. Five players came in on loan including three young goalkeepers who would all be used as the season progressed, England U19, U20 and U21 player Christian Walton came from Brighton and performed very well for 33 games and when he was recalled by his club in January he had conceded the lowest number of goals in the Division.

He was replaced by Matt Macey from Arsenal who played 13 games before he too was recalled by his club after an injury to Petr Cech in April. The season was completed by Stuart Moore on loan from Reading. Former youth full-back Luton born James Justin began to feature prominently making 39 appearances in all competition and winning an England U20 cap

There were three stand-out perfomances in the league, a home win against Wycombe Wanderers 4-1 with a Danny Hylton hat-trick put Luton top of the table, with my brother I watched an away win 4-0 at Yeovil which was some consolation for the previous seasons soaking and a 4-1 win at Accrington also stood out. Luton were never below 7th in the table but despite being undefeated in the last seven games there were just too many draws (seventeen) to finish any better than 4th well adrift of the top three. It would be play-off time again. In the FA Cup there was a good away win at Exeter 3-1 and a 6-2 crushing of Solihull Moors at Kenilworth Road before a 2-1 exit at Accrington.

The EFL Cup (they couldn't find a sponsor this year) saw two home ties with the Hatters disposing of Aston Villa 3-1 before going down to Leeds United 1-0. The EFL Trophy had a new sponsor, Checkatrade and a new format with group stages and the involvement of U21 teams from some Premier League and Championship teams. In the group stages Luton beat Gillingham and West Bromwich U21 but lost to Millwall. They still qualified for the next stage when Swindon Town were beaten 3-2 away. Then came three home ties with wins against Chesterfield 4-0 and Yeovil 5-2 before a narrow defeat to Oxford 3-2 in the semi-final.

All this had been done with yet another new sponsor's name on the orange shirts, this time in a two year deal it was Indian owned, South Korean motor company *SsangYong* with *Puma* replacing *Fila* as manufacturer.

The last and most important business of the season was the League 2 play-offs and Luton's opponents were Blackpool. Luton had beaten the Tangerines home and away in the league keeping clean sheets on both occasions and had finished seven points ahead of them in the table. What could possibly go wrong? The first leg was at Bloomfield Road which, watching on TV, seemed eerily empty due to many home supporters boycotting the game in protest against the owners. In front of just 3,882 spectators with home support outnumbered Blackpool went ahead after 19 minutes but goals from Dan Potts and Isaac Vassell a couple of minutes apart around the half-hour mark gave Luton a half-time lead. With a goal just after the break and another from a 67th minute penalty Blackpool took the match 3-2 with a hat-trick from Luton's top scorer of two seasons previous, Mark Cullen. In the return at Kenilworth Road Blackpool opened the scoring on 22 minutes but a Mellor own-goal and one from Scott Cuthbert on the stroke of half-time put the scores level on aggregate. Danny Hyton put a penalty away in the second half but Blackpool scored again and extra-time was looming when five minutes into added time, Luton's Jordan Cook made a headed goal line clearance which hit the back of keeper Stuart Moore and trickled over the line for a winner. Disappointment again, it seems that Luton just don't do play-offs!

SEASON 2017-18

It seemed that Nathan Jones had also decided that Luton don't do play-offs so automatic promotion was the target and that target was achieved in some style. Ten players were allowed to leave including Craig Machail-Smith, Stephen O'Donnell and Isaac Vassell. The same number came in pre-season with two more on loan and such was the strength of these players that eight of them would become virtually permanent fixtures in the team. Another strength of these players was that unlike so often in the past, only one was over thirty and five were under 25 years old. Defensive player Jack Stacey (45 appearances) came from Reading, Ireland U21 striker James Collins (45 appearances and 20 goals) from Crawley, Czech international goalkeeper Mareck Stech (42 appearances) from Sparta Prague, Elliot Lee (38 appearances) back from Barnsley, forward Harry Cornick (41 appearances) from Birmingham City, striker Luke Berry (39 appearances and 8 goals) from Cambridge United, Scotland international defender Andrew Shinnie (34 appearances) from Birmingham and back-up goalkeeper James Shea from AFC Wimbledon. If you add to this list the existing players Olly Lee, Danny Hylton, Glen Rea and Alan Sheehan who all made over 40 appearances you get some idea of how settled the team was.

The scene was set in the first game of the season at Kenilworth Road when going a goal down to Yeovil, Town came back to win 8-2 with a James Collins hat-trick. There was a 7-1 win over Stevenage with a Luke Berry hat-trick and Danny Hylton also netted three in the 7-0 beating of Cambridge.

My Christmas treat was a Boxing Day trip to Swindon to see the Hatters win 5-0. Town went top of the table on 21st November and stayed there until 10th March but they slipped when in a nervy spell between 24th February and 17th March they went five games without a win and we all got the jitters. But on 21st April Olly Lee scored at Brunton Park to draw 1-1 with Carlisle and guarantee automatic promotion. Luton never dropped below 2nd in the run-in but there was to be no catching champions Accrington Stanley who made it to the third tier for the first time in their history.

The FA Cup saw a 1-0 win at home to Portsmouth and then a 5-0 away win at Gateshead with five different scorers for Town but in Round 3 there was a 3-1 defeat away to Newcastle United. The League Cup had found sponsors and was now called the Carabao Cup. (Apparently it's an energy drink) but Luton couldn't find the energy to beat Ipswich at home going down 2-0. The Checkatrade Trophy still had the same format despite no-one seeming to be in favour of it. In the group stage Luton beat Spurs U21 on penalties after a 2-2 draw, Barnet on penalties after a 1-1 draw and AFC Wimbledon 2-1. In the second round West Ham U21 were knocked out 4-0 but after 0-0 at full time against Peterborough at Kenilworth Road, Luton lost on penalties 7-6.

175

SEASON 2018-19 AND BEYOND

Chairman Nick Owen stepped down on 3rd August 2017 and became a Vice-President of the club which reminded me that when Luton Town FC 2020 was formed in probably our darkest hour, it was called that because the stated aim of the consortium was to have the Hatters back in the top two tiers of English football by the year 2020.

Well they are pretty much on course, may soon at last have a new stadium to perform in and who knows? That's the great thing, we don't. Rochdale once spent 36 years in the same division and I calculate that in the past 36 years Luton have changed football tiers eleven times. I know which I would rather follow.

TOP ALL TIME APPEARANCES

	L	N	FAC	LC	O	TOT
Fred Hawkes (1900-20)	2	504	40	0	79	625
Bob Morton (1948-64)	495	0	48	7	12	562
Ricky Hill (1976-89)	436	0	33	38	1	508
Brian Stein (1977-88 & 91-92)	427	0	31	35	3	496
Mal Donaghy (1978-88 & 89-90)	415	0	36	34	3	488
Gordon Turner (1950-64)	408	0	25	7	12	450
Marvin Johnson (1988-02)	372	0	21	29	17	439
Ron Baynham (1952-65)	388	0	31	5	10	434
Syd Owen (1947-59)	388	0	27	0	8	423
Bob Hawkes (1901-20)	0	349	35	0	26	410
David Preece (1984-95)	336	0	27	23	9	395
Matthew Spring (1997-04 & 07-08)	308	0	24	20	5	357
Fred White (1900-09)	0	237	21	0	45	304
Jake Howells (2008-16)	29	191	25	0	31	276
Herbert Moody (1907-12)	0	232	15	0	19	266
Tim Breacker (1984-90)	210	0	21	24	7	262
Les Sealey (1983-89)	207	0	28	21	3	259
Bill McCurdy (1899-1910)	31	162	18	0	40	251
Mark Tyler (2009-16)	0	199	12	0	19	230
Mick Harford (1984-90)	168	0	27	17	5	217
Steve Foster (1984-89)	163	0	27	20	2	212

L League, NL Non-League, FAC FA Cup, LC League Cup O Other TOT Total
Years relate to time in first team rather than period with club

TOP ALL TIME GOAL SCORERS

	L	N	FAC	LC	O	TOT	
Gordon Turner (1950-64)		243	0	18	4	11	276
Andy Rennie (1926-34)		147	0	15	0	0	162
Brian Stein (1977-88 & 91-92)		130	0	6	15	3	154
Ernie Simms (1913-22)		47	62	13	0	8	130
Herbert Moody (1907-12)		0	86	11	0	9	106
Steve Howard (2001-06)		96	0	5	2	0	103
David Moss (1978-85)		88	0	3	3	0	94
Jimmy Yardley (1927-32)		78	0	16	0	0	94
Mick Harford (1984-90)		69	0	10	10	3	92
Joe Payne (1934-38)		83	0	4	0	0	87
Tony Thorpe (1992-99 & 02-03)		70	0	3	6	5	84
Syd Reid 69 (1922-28)		69	0	10	10	3	81
Hugh Billington (1938-48)		63	0	7	0	0	70
Geo. Stephenson (1934-39)		58	0	5	0	6	69
John O'Rourke (1963-66)		64	0	2	0	0	66
Ricky Hill (1976-89)		54	0	6	5	0	65
Allan Brown (1957-61)		51	0	6	0	1	58
Arthur Wileman (1912-15)		0	42	5	0	11	58
Malcolm McDonald (1969-70)		49	0	5	4	0	58
Andre Gray (2012-14)		0	52	2	0	3	57
Tommy Tait (1931-33)		50	0	7	0	0	57
Bob Morton (1948-64)		48	0	4	0	3	55
Phil Gray (1991-93 & 97-00)		43	0	4	6	0	53
Bruce Rioch (1964-69)		47	0	2	3	0	52

SOURCES

Luton Town Football Club The Full Record: Roger Wash & Simon Pitts 2nd Edition 2014

Completely Top Hatters: Dean P Hayes 2002

The Definitive Luton Town FC: Steve Bailey 1997

Football League Players' Records: Michael Joyce 2004

Hatters Heroes: Roger Walsh 2008

The Luton Town Story 1885-1995: Timothy Collings 1985

Luton Town FC's 50 Greatest Players: Paul Rance 2012

The Times 50 Best Luton Players Of All Time: Denis O'Donaghue

thestrawplaiters.com

footballandthefirstworldwar.org

hugmansfootballers.com

worldwar1luton.com

world warIIluton.com

wikipedia.org

My own fading memory

ABOUT THE AUTHOR

George Jackson was born in Houghton Regis, Bedfordshire and has in various lives been a Scientific Civil Servant with the Meteorological Office, a Police Officer, a Pub Landlord and a Town Clerk but throughout those varied lives he has remained a true Hatters fan. Work took him away from Bedfordshire in his teens so following Luton Town has for the most part been from a distance in the last nearly sixty years but no less devoted for that.

His early life is described in his autobiography *From Country Boy To Weather Man* published by The Book Castle, Dunstable in 2006 (now out of print) and growing up in Houghton Regis, working for the Met Office and his police service in Huntingdonshire and Pembrokeshire is covered in *My First Four Lives* published by and available on Amazon.

Printed in Great Britain
by Amazon